Ten
Steps
to Increase
Jobsite
Productivity

James J. Adrian
Ph.D., PE, CPA

A Service of
NAHB

BuilderBooks™
National Association of Home Builders
1201 15th Street, NW
Washington, DC 20005-2800
www.builderbooks.com

Ten Steps to Increase Jobsite Productivity
James J. Adrian, Ph.D, PE, CPA

ISBN 0-86718-523-6

Cataloging-in-Publication Data available from the Library of Congress

Cover design by Armen Kojoyian

Disclaimer
This publication is designed to provide accurate and authoritative information in regard to the subject matter covered. It is sold with the understanding that the publisher is not engaged in rendering legal, accounting, or other professional service. If legal advice or other expert assistance is required, the services of a competent professional person should be sought.
—From a Declaration of Principles jointly adopted by a Committee of the American Bar Association and a Committee of Publishers and Associations.

For further information, please contact:
BuilderBooks™
National Association of Home Builders
1201 15th Street, NW
Washington, DC 20005-2800
(800) 223-2665
Check us out online at: www.builderbooks.com

11/01 Circle Graphics/P.A. Hutchison 1500

Contents

List of Figures

About the Author

James J. Adrian, Ph.D., PE, CPA, is a recognized worldwide expert on the measurement and improvement of construction productivity. Through his work as a professor of Civil Engineering and Construction at Bradley University, the Associated General Contractors named Dr. Adrian National Construction Educator of the Year in 1996. As president of Adrian International LLC and Construction Systems Co., he provides consulting services to the construction industry and residential builders. He has been the author of a bimonthly newsletter titled *Improving Construction Productivity* for nineteen years. Dr. Adrian can be reached at 5317 N. Woodview Ave., Peoria, IL 61614.

Acknowledgments

I am grateful to my wife, Sandy, for once again providing me an environment in which I have been able to serve others through my work and writings. I have developed many of my ideas and procedures described in this book during my Ph.D. thesis many years ago at the University of Illinois-Urbana and as a construction industry consultant on productivity for more than twenty-five years. I am indebted to the many practitioners in the construction industry for the knowledge that I have accumulated. This has been an invaluable in my preparation of this book.

Ten Steps to Increase Jobsite Productivity was produced under the general direction of NAHB staff members Greg French, Staff Vice President, Publications and Non-dues Revenues; Eric Johnson, Publisher, BuilderBooks; Theresa Minch, Acquisitions Editor; David Rhodes, Art and Production Director; and Toral Patel, Assistant Editor.

Introduction to Productivity Improvement

The residential builder is in a very competitive business. Given the large number of firms in the business, the amount of profit margin the residential builder earns on a single project or residential unit is relatively small. Small errors or a decrease in project productivity relative to the bid can eliminate any planned profit. It follows that the key to being a profitable residential builder is to seek a means of increasing jobsite productivity.

Productivity, or the lack of it, is perhaps the number one problem confronting the construction industry, the residential firm, and the construction project. In this chapter, we will discuss how the residential builder can measure its productivity and its ability or opportunity to increase productivity.

Productivity can be viewed as the efficiency by which materials are placed by labor and equipment. Productivity is commonly measured by means of the following definition:

$$\text{Productivity} = \frac{\text{Units or Dollars of Output (adjusted for inflation)}}{\text{Person-hours of Input or Effort}}$$

It should be noted that while this is a widely accepted definition, it can be misleading because person-hours is in the denominator. This might lead one to believe that the only way to increase productivity is to work harder, to make more labor effort. In this book, we will illustrate that there are many ways to increase construction productivity that do not center on working harder. We will focus on increasing productivity via working smarter and by improving management practices.

A second point should be made regarding the above definition of productivity. Given the definition, productivity for various construction work tasks may be given as cubic yards of concrete placed per person-hour, board feet of lumber placed per person-hour, etc. However, it should be noted that individuals in the construction industry, and in particular the estimator, normally speak of person-hours per unit instead of units per person-hour. As such, it is more common for the estimator to be citing the reciprocal of productivity.

Low Construction Industry Productivity

Given the prior definition of productivity, the U.S. Department of Commerce has measured the average annual increases in construction industry productivity to be less than 1 percent a year for the last 10 years. The average annual increase in construction productivity of 0.8 percent compares to a 2 percent to 3 percent annual increase for all U.S. industries.

Unfortunately, during the same time period when construction productivity has been nearly flat, the residential builder's construction costs have risen. During the past 10 to 15 years, construction costs have increased each year, sometimes in excess of 5 percent in a given year. This increasing cost and relatively flat productivity has put downward pressure on the profitability of many residential building firms. Given the fierce competition of the bidding process, firms may not be able to pass on added material and labor costs to the customer. For many contracting firms, this decreasing profitability—owing to the failure to increase productivity while costs have increased—has resulted in the risk of the bid exceeding the planned profitability in the bid. This is illustrated in Figure I-1.

Accounting and estimating studies have indicated that on the average, a residential builder brings in a project for a 6 percent different cost than estimated independent of change orders. This is illustrated in Figure I-1. However, increasing costs and relatively small productivity increases have resulted in many firms having their profit margins (after company overhead) decrease to approximately 2 percent. This fact is evidenced by published financial ratio as

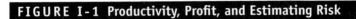

FIGURE I-1 Productivity, Profit, and Estimating Risk

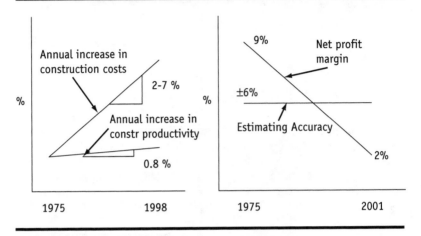

reported by RMA Financial Ratios for Commercial Construction (RMA Annual Statement Studies, Robert Morris Associates).

Inflation of costs can be addressed two ways by the residential builder: 1) by holding down costs or 2) by increasing productivity. The residential builder has not done well in either of these and as such one can argue that the cost of construction relative to the value of work put in place has decreased significantly.

Another way of looking at productivity in the construction industry is to look at the composition of the eight-hour workday. Documented jobsite studies indicate that between 40 percent and 60 percent of a typical construction day is taken up by nonproductive time. Nonproductive time can include time associated with workers waiting for instructions, doing redo work, taking advantage of a lack of proper supervision, etc. In addition, nonproductive time includes a certain amount of what can be referred to as "unnecessary support time" such as a worker carrying boards from one location to another merely because the material was not effectively stored in the proper location provided in the jobsite layout. An example of such a workday is illustrated in Figure I-2. Especially noteworthy is the fact that the author's studies indicate that approximately one-third of nonproductive time can be traced to management actions (or lack of actions).

Inspection of Figure I-2 indicates nonproductive time relates to causes such as poor communications; waiting for material, labor, or

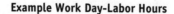

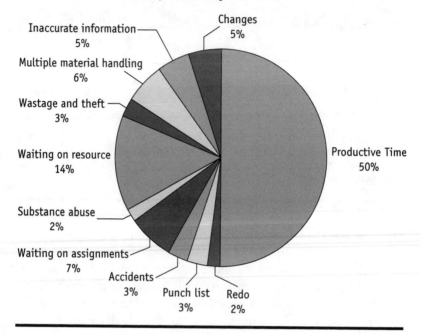

FIGURE I-2 Productivity Defects at the Jobsite

Example Work Day-Labor Hours

equipment; late starts and early quits, etc. These causes of nonproductive time cannot be blamed on labor attitudes or labor work rules. Simply put, they are the fault of management and can be corrected by improved jobsite management. Hundreds of thousands, if not millions, of dollars of work are performed each year that can be traced to poor communications. The project supervisor tells the worker what to do, and the worker may do the work incorrectly because what the supervisor said is not what the worker heard. In addition, the fact that the worker may always be told what to do rather than asked for ideas can lead to a counterproductive worker attitude.

Opportunity to Increase Productivity

It is not being suggested that the solution to the problem of low construction industry productivity or nonproductive time is an easy problem to address. The construction process is a difficult one. Problems such as a variable environment (precipitation and temperature variations) and the complexity of the building process itself are just a few of the issues that most non-construction industries do not have to confront.

Independent of the difficulties associated with improving construction productivity, it should be pointed out that tremendous opportunity exists to improve productivity. If the construction process can be correctly identified as having 50 percent nonproductive time, it also can be rephrased as having an opportunity to increase productivity by 50 percent.

It is unrealistic to believe that the supervisor for a residential builder can eliminate all construction nonproductive time. However, a mere small increase in productivity on the order of 5 percent can have a significant impact on the profitability of the residential builder. Figure I-3 shows a breakdown of a typical construction bid for a residential building project.

A 5 percent increase in productivity would have the effect of decreasing the overall project labor costs by 5 percent. As illustrated in Figure I-3, a 5 percent increase in productivity and a corresponding 5 percent decrease in labor costs would result in a profit

FIGURE I-3 Impact of Productivity on Profits

EXAMPLE PROJECT

Bid Cost Component	Cost %	Example Project	$200,000
Direct Labor Cost	40	$80,000	
Direct Material Cost	35	70,000	
Construction Equipment Cost	7	14,000	
General Conditions-Job Overhead	8	16,000	
Company Overhead Cost	8	16,000	
Net Profit	2	4,000	
TOTAL	100	$200,000	

Assume a 5% Increase in Labor Productivity
The result: Labor Cost Savings = (5%) ($8,000) = $4,000
note: A 5% increase doubles the "planned" profits

Assume a 5% Decrease in Labor Productivity
The result: Labor Cost Increase = (5%) ($8,000) = $4,000
note: A 5% decrease eliminates the "planned" profits

contribution equal to the initial planned profit. The end result is that a mere 5 percent increase in productivity can result in doubling the profits of the residential builder. Naturally, it also follows that a 5 percent decrease in actual productivity versus planned productivity would eliminate any planned profits in the bid shown in Figure I-3.

Another way of looking at the opportunity for improving productivity and the positive impact of such an effort is to look at the potential impact of the construction supervisor. Previously, it was noted that on many projects, one-third of the nonproductive time at the jobsite can be traced to the lack of onsite management actions. Given this assumption, and given a typical cost breakdown for a $200,000 project as illustrated in Figure I-4, one can suggest that one-third of $40,000, or $13,333, can be traced to poor management or a lack of management.

Assuming that the supervisor for a residential builder can implement effective management practices that will eliminate the nonproductive time related to management practices, it follows that the effective supervisor can enable an additional $13,333 profits, a number that is more than three times the initially planned profit in the bid estimate. There are few industries in which a supervisor can make such an impact on the profitability of the firm. Clearly, a supervisor can make a big difference in the construction process!

It should be pointed out that in Figures I-3 and I-4, the benefits of improved productivity may actually be somewhat higher than those calculated. If productivity is improved, the project duration is likely to decrease. Given the fact that job overhead costs, such as trailer rental and supervision costs, are almost completely proportional to project duration, it follows that an increase in productivity also would lessen job overhead costs, resulting in additional contributions to project profits. The end result is that a small increase in jobsite productivity can result in a significant increase in jobsite profitability.

In the following 10 chapters, we will outline a 10-step program to increase jobsite productivity and improve the time, cost, quality, and safety of the residential builder's projects. The ultimate objective of the program is to increase the residential builder's profitability.

FIGURE I-4 Impact of Improved Supervision at the Jobsite

PREMISE 1: Example Cost Breakdown of $200,000 Residential Project

Direct Labor Cost	$80,000
Direct Material Cost	70,000
Direct Equipment Cost	14,000
General Conditions (Job Overhead)	16,000
Company Overhead	16,000
Profit	4,000
TOTAL	**$200,000**

PREMISE 2: Typical Nonproductive Labor Cost in Bid

Productive Time	50%	$40,000
Nonproductive Time	50%	$40,000

PREMISE 3: Reasons for Nonproductive Time

Labor related	1/3	$13,333
Industry related	1/3	$13,333
Management decisions related	1/3	$13,333

PREMISE 4: Possible Impact of Good Supervisor
Assume an effective supervisor can eliminate nonproductive time related to management actions or inactions

Result/Conclusion

Decrease in labor cost	$13,333

Possible return of an effective supervisor

Decrease in labor cost / Profit in bid = $13,333 / $4,000 = 3.33

Conclusion:
An effective supervisor can more than triple the planned job profits.

A Ten Step Program to Improve Project Productivity and Company Profits

In the following chapters, the 10-step program, or "10 Steps to Increase Jobsite Productivity," will be presented.

1. Preplanning a Productive Jobsite
2. Managing People: Making a Job Look Like a Firm

3. Practical Planning and Scheduling
4. Implementing an Effective Control System
5. Eliminating Productivity Defects at the Project
6. Implementing "MORE" Productivity
7. Managing Equipment for Productivity Improvement
8. Managing Subcontractors
9. Managing Change Orders and Disputes
10. A Safe Job is a Productive Job

Pre-Planning a Productive Project

From the residential builder's view, a project is successful if it meets the following four criteria:

- Constructed on the financial budget
- Constructed according to the project duration schedule
- The project meets quality objectives
- The project is completed safely (i.e. free of injuries)

To meet the four criteria, the construction supervisor must be attentive to what might be considered the four phases of the construction project. These phases are shown in Figure 1-1.

Much emphasis is given to the estimating phase of the construction phase of the project. Given that most construction contracts

FIGURE 1-1 Four Phases of a Construction Project

	Estimating/ Bidding	Pre-Planning	Construction Phase	Close-Out Phase
Bad	"wild enthusiasm	"often dormant"	"leads to fire drill"	"leads to disputes/ litigation"
Good	"realistic enthusiasm"	"pro-active planning"	"cost, time, quality, safety success	"celebration"

Project Letting   Start Construction   Project Completed

are awarded based on a "low bid" bidding process, the importance of the estimate is obvious.

The importance of the construction phase stems from its visibility. The residential builder operates out in the open and the visibility of labor and equipment at a project puts the construction phase and the supervisor under a magnifying glass.

However, the success of a project when it comes to cost, time, quality, and safety is in great part dependent on what the supervisor does or does not do prior to the construction phase. All too often the residential builder puts a project to rest during the time period between when they get the contract and when the firm starts construction. The firm and the supervisor do very little during this time period. In fact, the supervisor may not even be assigned to manage the project until a few days before the project starts. The result is that there may be little to no preplanning of project tasks such as planning production budgets, preordering long-lead material items, and organizing the paper flow for the project. In effect, the project becomes dormant between project letting and the start of construction. As noted in Figure 1-1, this leads to the construction process being in a fire-drill mode—a process of reacting to problems that may have been prevented through the process of preplanning. These problems can lead to project disputes, claims, cost overruns, time overruns, etc.

As illustrated in Figure 1-1, preplanning can lead to a more productive construction phase and a more desirable project closeout. The point is that productivity improvement starts before the construction phase; it starts with getting the supervisor involved in preplanning prior to the start of the construction phase.

The preplanning phase of a project should focus on two objectives:

1. Interfacing the construction supervisor with the estimate
2. Planning the construction phase

Suggested preplanning tasks for each of these objectives are presented in the following sections.

Interfacing the Supervisor with the Estimate

Most residential builders structure the estimating function as a decentralized process; the firm establishes a separate department and assigns individuals to this function. These individuals become full-time estimators. This decentralized estimating process is illustrated in Figure 1-2.

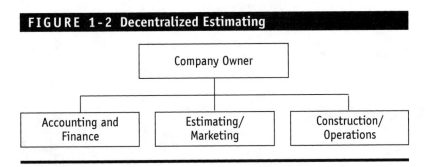

FIGURE 1-2 Decentralized Estimating

The decentralized estimating process benefits the residential builder because the estimators become specialized in costing work, securing subcontractor bids, buying out materials, etc. The construction supervisor becomes focused on the constructing of the project. However, there also is a major disadvantage of the process. If the bid/estimate prepared by the estimator is successful, the project is "handed off" to the supervisor. For one, the supervisor may not get the opportunity to provide valuable construction knowledge to the estimator. Secondly, the construction supervisor gets very little information about the estimating assumptions and contract document information. This puts the supervisor at a disadvantage in regard to planning and carrying out the construction process.

One of the purposes of the preplanning phase of the project is to interface the construction supervisor with the project estimate in order to provide input to the estimate and to learn valuable information from the prepared estimate and accompanying contract documents.

A recommended process for interfacing the project supervisor into the estimating phase of the project is shown in Figure 1-3.

The process shown in Figure 1-3 includes the following five steps:

1. The supervisor should meet with the estimator during bid preparation and provides construction productivity information to the estimator.

The construction estimator often comes under attack for not having sufficient knowledge or experience in the construction

FIGURE 1-3 Overview of Preplanning Steps

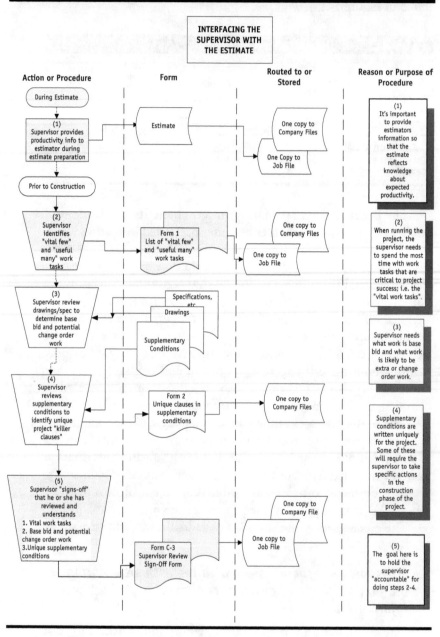

process to properly estimate labor and equipment cost and productivity. By reviewing the project drawings and specifications with the estimator, the supervisor can provide valuable insights regarding unique work difficulties and can suggest work methods that influence the costing of the project work. The purpose here is to have the estimator and supervisor merge their knowledge into an estimate/bid that reflects what the project will cost when it is built under the direction of the supervisor.

Secondly, if a project goes over the time or cost budget in the construction phase of a project, it is common for the estimator to blame the construction supervisor, and for the construction supervisor to blame the estimator. By having the supervisor provide input during the estimate preparation, the issue of who is responsible for budget overruns is removed because the estimate and construction phases become more of a team effort. Everyone gains from this team effort rather than blaming one another.

Some of the input the supervisor can provide to the estimator during the bidding phase of the project includes the following:

- Information as to what methods of construction should be used; for example, what forming systems should be used. If the estimator assumes one forming system and the supervisor uses a different forming system to construct the project, surely the cost of doing the work will be different than the bid.
- Knowledge about unique construction difficulties that may influence the costing of the project.
- Knowledge about likely labor, material, or equipment shortages that may influence the costing of the project.
- Suggestions regarding the project time schedule (e.g. how it might be shortened) that may influence the costing of time-related costs, including general conditions costs.

One of the problems with formalizing the estimating process by having the supervisor meet and provide input to the estimator is that some construction firms may not assign a specific supervisor to manage a project until after the estimate is bid and the contract is awarded the firm. Having the residential builder identify the likely supervisor early in the four-phase process shown earlier can alleviate this organizational problem. Even if a supervisor is working on another project at the time a prospective project is being estimated, the supervisor could be called in to meet with the estimator for a few hours. The purpose of the meeting is not to prepare the estimate, but rather to provide input into it. This is not a major time consuming task.

2. The supervisor should review the estimate to identify the "vital few" work tasks and the "useful many" work tasks.

As pointed out in section one, the construction supervisor seldom has enough time to do everything expected of him or her once the project starts. They cannot be everywhere every minute of the day. For example, once the project starts, there are likely several work tasks happening simultaneously at the project—forming walls at one location, rough carpentry framing at another, specialty work at another location, etc.

Because the supervisor cannot be everywhere every minute of the construction workday, he or she must pick and choose. To optimize the supervision function, the supervisor should be more attentive to supervising important work tasks; i.e. the "vital few" activities. On any one project, the supervisor may have to monitor tens, if not hundreds, of work tasks or cost codes. However, it is likely that no more than a handful of these work tasks in great part dictate the project time, cost, quality, and safety.

Four criteria are suggested for identifying project vital few work tasks:

A. Cost of the work
B. Risk or variation in the production process
C. Work tasks that dictate or drive the project schedule
D. Work tasks the firm and supervisor have seldom done previously

A. Cost of the work

If the supervisor cannot be in two places at the same time, he or she should be supervising the more expensive work tasks. For example, all other things being equal, if a work task, such as excavation work, costs $6 per cubic yard to perform, and the placing of concrete costs $60 per cubic yard to perform, the supervisor should spend more of his or her time managing the $60 task.

B. Risk or variation in the production process

Risk simply means variation from an expected estimate or average. Assume a supervisor is using two different framing methods at two different locations at a project. Assume further that the residential builder has gathered hourly productivity data about each of the work methods as shown in Figure 1-4.

Observation of the data shown in Figure 1-4 indicates that on average the workers using the two different faming methods are obtaining the same average productivity (foot board measure of framing per person hour). However, there is considerably more variation in the hourly productivity for method 2. There were hours when the crew did very well (above average), and hours when the crew did very poor (below average). Given a choice between two places, the supervisor should spend more supervision on work method 2.

Consider the two work tasks of forming concrete walls and placing the concrete into the walls with a ready-mix truck and a chute. A review of project results would indicate that actual craft-hours expended to form the walls often vary considerably from the estimated craft-hours; i.e. it is a high-risk function. On the other hand, a review of project results would indicate that the actual craft-hours taken to

FIGURE 1-4 Hourly Productivity Data for Two Work Methods

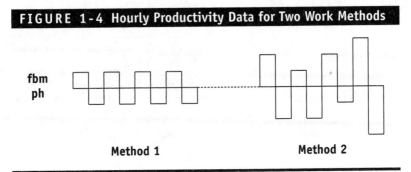

fbm ph

Method 1   Method 2

place the concrete is very close to the budgeted or estimated craft-hours. However, more often than not, the placement gets more supervision time than the concrete forming work task. The supervisor needs to access how he or she spends their limited supervision time.

C. **Work tasks that dictate or drive the project schedule**

One of the purposes of preparing an overall project schedule (such as a bar chart or critical path schedule) is to determine which work tasks or activities dictate or drive the project duration, often referred to as the "critical path." Clearly these work tasks or activities should get more attention from the supervisor than so called noncritical activities; e.g. work tasks that have time "float." While focusing on critical path activities is important, it should be noted that it is only one of the four criteria for identifying vital few work tasks. A later chapter focuses more on the use of planning tools, such as the critical path method, to increase productivity.

D. **Work tasks the firm and supervisor have seldom done previously.**

Typically, on each and every project a supervisor manages, he or she has to monitor one of two types of work: 1) work the firm and the supervisor have frequently performed on other projects or 2) new work tasks that the firm and the supervisor have not done before. The supervisor needs to be more attentive to work that he or she has little prior experience.

For example, some residential builders do their own masonry work, and others subcontract this work. If a general contractor decides to take on the masonry work as a means of being more competitive, the supervisor needs to pay more attention to this work on the project in question. The new work, and lack of experience performing it, is likely to provide more potential for surprises (good or bad) than work the firm has performed previously.

Using these four criteria, the construction supervisor should identify these vital few work tasks prior to starting the project, i.e. preplanning. These vital few work tasks need more attention in regard to planning and control. For example, the supervisor might decide to monitor the above-mentioned masonry work on a daily basis by measuring the blocks or brick put in place per crew. On the other hand, the supervisor might rely more on a weekly or monthly job cost report as a means of monitoring the "useful many" work tasks.

3. Supervisor reviews contract drawings and specifications to determine base bid work and potential change order work.

The typical gap between the estimating and supervising functions can lead to the supervisor performing extra construction work and not billing the work or collecting money for the work. The construction industry performs thousands, if not millions, of dollars of work every year for free due to the fact that the supervisor may not thoroughly understand the scope of the base bid work prior to starting the project. The result may be that the supervisor ends up doing work that he or she believes is base bid work, when in fact it could be billed as extra or change order work. To prevent this, the supervisor should review project drawings and specifications thoroughly prior to starting construction.

Change order work—work not required as base bid work and not included in the contractor estimate—typically occurs during construction and can be disruptive to the construction process. Poorly administered change order work is one of the leading reasons for construction disputes between the contractor and the project owner and/or designer. The change order work process is typically a three-step process:

1. Project owner and/or designer issues a request for change
2. Residential builder prepares a cost proposal (CP) for performing the extra work
3. Project owner, through the designer, issues a change order for the work

Unfortunately, each of these three steps does not always go smoothly. Sometimes the project owner and the residential builder cannot agree that the work in question is actually extra or change order work; the owner/designer may take the position that the work should be considered base bid work, while the contractor argues that it is extra work. Secondly, they may not be able to agree on a fair price for the work. As a result, disputes may evolve.

The contractor and supervisor need to be proactive in regard to change orders. If the supervisor can identify change order work early, he or she is in a better position to negotiate a fair price for the work and also can take appropriate management actions to minimize the potential impact on project productivity and the project schedule.

A review of project drawings and specifications should be made by the supervisor to identify potential work difficulties and potential extra work areas. Rather than reacting to extra work situations during the construction process, a supervisor should attempt to identify them prior to the project so that he or she can properly manage the situation.

As part of the contract document review of drawings and specifications, it is recommended that the supervisor fill out a form with potential work difficulties and potential extra work that may evolve. This will serve as a good reminder once the construction process starts.

4. *Review project supplementary conditions to identify unique project clauses that may cause the supervisor difficulties if they are overlooked. Given the potential detrimental impact of these clauses, they are often referred to as "killer clauses."*

When a construction contract is signed, the residential builder agrees to abide by the following six legal contract documents:

1. Drawings
2. Specifications
3. General Conditions
4. Supplementary Conditions
5. Addendum
6. Agreement Form

The **drawings** essentially indicate the quantity of work that must be performed by the residential builder, square feet of contact area of wall forms that must be erected, board feet of framing, linear feet of pipe, pounds of ductwork, etc.

Specifications focus more on the quality of work that has to be achieved—compaction of the excavation work, concrete strength, etc. Obviously, it is important that the supervisor understand both the drawings and specifications so that the quantity and quality of the work is performed according to the contract.

General conditions are, by definition, rather general. The document states the roles and responsibilities of the general contractor, the subcontractor, the designer, etc. For the most part, the general conditions are the same on each and every project.

The **addendum** represents changes that are made in the contract documents prior to the letting of the contract. They are like change orders except they occur prior to the letting as opposed to after the contract letting.

The **agreement** form is the document on which the residential builder and the project owner agree to a dollar amount to do the contract work.

It is the **supplementary** conditions that often are overlooked (unread) by the residential builder and construction supervisor. The supplementary conditions are sometimes referred to as the "special conditions."

It is critical that the supervisor become acquainted with the supplementary conditions prior to starting the construction process. In the supplementary conditions, the project designer writes contract administration clauses that may be unique and may be detrimental to the supervisor's ability to manage the construction process in a manner he or she is accustomed to.

The owner or project designer may attempt to overprotect the project owner with various protective clauses. Given the existence of these clauses, the residential builder may have taken specific actions in order to minimize the potential impact of the clause. A few of the clauses that need the supervisor's attention are shown in Figure 1-5.

There may be several other supplementary condition clauses that the contractor and supervisor need to know about such

FIGURE 1-5   Clauses that Need Supervisor's Attention

Supplementary conditions clause	What it is	Implication to supervisor
Liquidated damage clause	Indicates financial damages (dollars per day) the contractor will be assessed if the project is not completed on time.	Needs to be especially attentive to completing project on time. Needs to document any and all delays that are caused by project owner or designer.
Notification clause	Requires the supervisor to put the project owner and/or designer on notice within a specific time period (e.g. 14 days) of an event if the contractor is to have any financial remedy for issue.	Needs to be more attentive to writing letters and notifying project owner and/or designer about a problem sooner than he or she may have in the past.
No damage for delay clause	If significant change orders occur, the contractor will likely be given additional project time (liquidated damages not assessed) but will not be given financial remedy for added general condition costs.	Needs to be especially attentive to completing project on time. Needs to document any and all delays that are caused by project owner or designer.

that he or she can take the appropriate action when managing the construction phase of the project. Because some of these clauses are unique to a specific project, they have the potential to "surprise" the supervisor after the fact while managing the construction phase of the project.

The use of the supplementary clause checklist can minimize the possibility of overlooking one of these clauses. Using such a checklist, the residential builder looks for the existence of such a clause when reviewing the supplementary conditions, records the existence or nonexistence, and takes appropriate actions. Obviously, it is possible that a new clause appears on a project. However, once it does, even if it is overlooked the first time, it should be added to the checklist such that it isn't missed a second time.

Just as it is important for the estimator to take-off project quantities from the drawings to determine required construction tasks, it also is important that the supervisor take-off unique supplementary conditions. Spending a small amount of time preplanning the project can result in minimizing difficulties during the construction phase of the project.

5. Supervisor should sign-off that preplanning tasks have been performed.

Given the many tasks that the supervisor has to do, it is possible that he or she may overlook an important preplanning task. The best way not forget something is to use a checklist.

Planning a Productive Jobsite Layout

One of the more important and often overlooked organization tasks of a construction supervisor is laying out the project site. Questions as to where to place trailers, where to store onsite materials, and where equipment should be located when not in use all necessitate decisions that are part of the site layout task.

All too often, a supervisor fails to analyze alternatives when it comes to the layout task. Instead, he or she somewhat haphazardly puts the trailer at one location, the material storage area at another, the subcontractor trailers at other locations, and so on. The supervisor may overlook the effect that the locations of these job-support components have on productivity, safety, worker satisfaction, and communications.

For a given project, there is one and only one optimal layout. If a job is planned on the basis of any other layout, some aspect of the working environment will be less than optimal. For example, if the materials storage location causes workers to continually walk long distances to get materials, hours of nonproductive labor time will result. Similarly, if materials are stored away from the place of their subsequent fabrication, they will need to be unnecessarily double lifted. Storing heavy equipment in the path of workers may increase the chance of injury. Placing a materials storage area in a location with no visual control or near the entrance or exit to the jobsite may promote theft.

Consider the example jobsite layout illustrated in Figure 1-6. It is not a productive layout because materials are stored too far from the fabrication area, the trailer is in an awkward place, and equipment is stored in a location that causes congestion and possible accidents.

The alternative jobsite layout illustrated in Figure 1-7 represents a significant improvement relative to the one shown in Figure 1-6. It will improve project productivity, communication, safety, and

FIGURE 1-6 An Unproductive Jobsite Layout

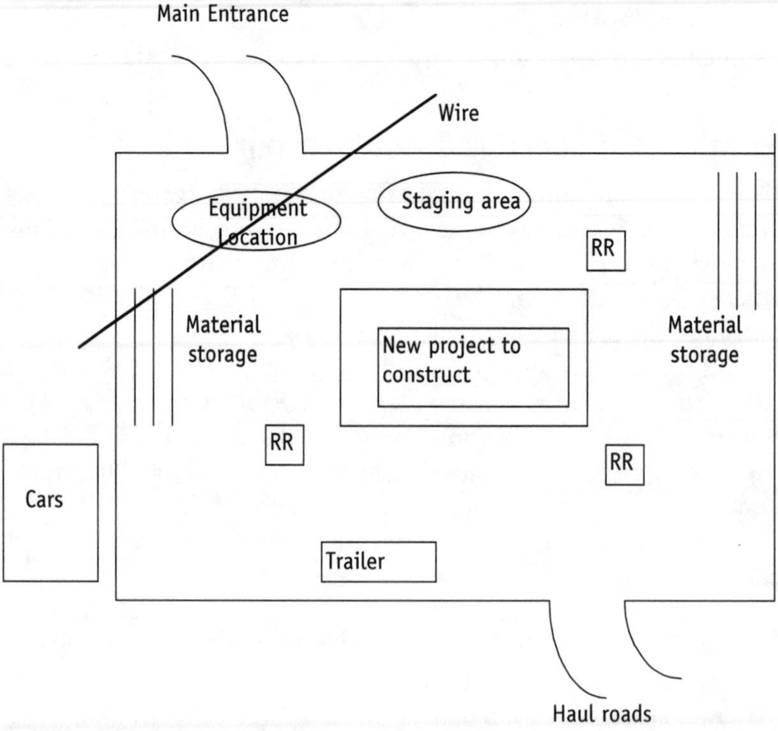

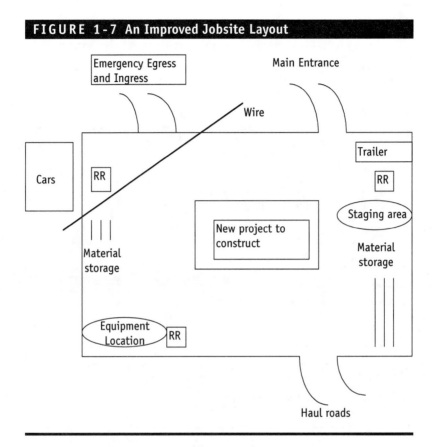

FIGURE 1-7 An Improved Jobsite Layout

minimize theft. By expending a few minutes of preplanning time, the jobsite layout can be improved.

A structured approach to the jobsite-layout task is needed. Such an approach should recognize "things" and "concerns." The things are various trailers, materials, equipment, storage areas, signs, lavatory locations, luncheon and break area locations, etc. Concerns include distances required to walk, safety, accounting controls, material or equipment theft, avoidance of adversarial human relations, and overall productivity enhancement.

A Preplanning Checklist

Just as a checklist can aid the supervisor in identifying "killer" clauses in the supplementary conditions, a preplanning checklist can aid the supervisor in making sure that he or she doesn't overlook an important preplanning task. A sample preplanning checklist is illustrated in Figure 1-8.

It is important that the residential builder use such a checklist on each and every project; he or she should not choose to use it on some

FIGURE 1-8 Pre-planning Checklist

Task	Name	Title	Date	Action to Take
Supervisor reviews drawings and specifications to determine base bid work, areas of difficulty, and potential change order work				
"Vital few" and "useful many" work tasks selected				
Review of supplementary conditions to identify unique or "killer" clauses				
Scheduling requirements				
Work coordination requirements				
Added safety requirements				
Added reporting requirements				
Unique meeting requirements				
Partnering requirements				
Clean-up requirements				
Long-lead items/materials				
Special equipment to requisition				
Change order process				
Utility interface requirements				
Unique labor requirements or rules				

projects, but not on others. Similarly, all the supervisors in the firm should use it (or if the firm decides not to use it, then no one should).

The residential building firm has to address the practice of using different forms and different procedures within the same firm. In many firms, some foremen are very attentive to doing good time-cards, while others do a poor job, including making cost code errors, writing illegibly, or failing to fill out the entire form. Similarly, some supervisors do a good job of completely filling out a daily report regarding work performed, weather, number of workers present, instructions given, etc. However, a few supervisors in the same firm may choose to be sloppy and tardy when filling out daily reports.

Quality can be defined as consistency. Once a firm sets up defined practices and procedures, everyone should follow them consistently. That is one of the advantages of using standardized forms and checklists such as the checklist shown on the following page.

Why should the residential builder be concerned about preplanning? If a supervisor is a good motivator and gets his workers to work hard, why should he or she follow set out procedures such as using the preplanning checklist on the following page? The answer is that it *does* matter. Inconsistent practices lead to a lack of accountability, an increased possibility of losing a lawsuit or claim, and perhaps most importantly, reduced construction productivity.

2

Managing People: Making a Job Look Like a Firm

The construction process is very dependent on the efforts of construction workers. Typically on projects, the direct labor cost component may be in excess of 35 to 40 percent of the total project cost (the other cost components being material, equipment, job overhead, and company overhead).

The residential builder may employ construction workers directly, i.e. perform self-performed work, or may employ subcontractors who employ construction workers (often called tradespersons). In many cases the residential builder will do both—self-performed work and subcontract work. The point remains that no matter if employed directly by the residential builder or through his or her subcontractors, the project can only be built on time and on budget through the productive efforts of onsite workers.

While considered a manufacturing industry, the construction industry can also be thought of as a service industry because of the high dependence on onsite labor efforts. This high dependence on labor efforts is compounded by the fact that many construction workers may view themselves as working for a job rather than a firm. A tool-and-die worker in a factory, a retail clerk at a store, or a receptionist at an office may work for a firm their entire working life, but a construction craftsman may work for several builders in a given year. One might argue that the construction worker doesn't view himself as working for firms; instead, he may view himself working on jobs.

The end result is that the residential builder and the supervisor are very dependent on the work attitude of the construction worker. A worker may have an attitude that he helps the firm by being productive when he doesn't have to be, or he may have an attitude that he won't be productive unless he has to be. For example, if a worker completes work assigned to him, does he go looking for more work to do, or does he stand idle waiting for more work to be assigned to him? The difference between a worker's attitude is in great part the difference between a productive, profitable job and a nonproductive, low-profit job. If the worker views himself as working for a firm, he is more likely to be productive when he doesn't have to versus if he views himself as working for a job.

Four Needs of a Worker

The fact that construction workers may view themselves as working for a job versus a firm compounds the personnel management efforts of the supervisor and the residential builder. In an attempt to develop positive worker attitudes and align the worker to the construction firm as well as the job, the author proposes that the supervisor pay attention to the following four needs of each and every worker:

1. Pride in work
2. A system for measuring performance
3. An effective communication channel
4. Monetary benefits

1. Pride in work

Pride in work in great part includes recognizing the workers and giving them a sense of accomplishment. Personnel management actions, such as a pat on the back, placing the names of workers on a sign at the jobsite, asking workers for suggestions and ideas, and having a day in which the workers are able to bring their children or friends to view the jobsite, can all be part of a long-term commitment to productivity improvement. While some of these and other personnel management actions are constrained by the short-term nature of some jobs and by other constraints like insurance requirements, failure to show an effort in giving workers pride in their work can yield negative results.

One way to give workers pride is to keep reminding them what is good about their projects, not what is bad.

Supervisors and workers cannot be effective unless they are proud of what they do. If the residential builder's supervisor is a whiner—always complaining, always blaming people—or projects an image that he or she doesn't like what he or she is doing, it can negatively impact the attitudes and productivity of the workers and the overall project.

The construction supervisor and his or her workers have every right to be proud of what they do. The construction industry is the backbone of the U.S. economy. Annually, new construction is in the range of 8 percent to 12 percent of the gross national product, much of which is new residential units. The industry employs more than five million people and, perhaps most importantly, the construction industry makes things; it doesn't simply trade things. Any economy that is to prosper over the long term has to make things.

The following is proposed:

The supervisor should make a daily effort to turn problems into opportunities. He or she should reduce incidents of blaming people and instead spend more time commending people and telling them what they did right rather than what they did wrong.

Let's take two supervisors that are confronted with the following problems:

- Five days of bad weather in a row
- A subcontractor that is not staffing the job with enough workers
- A project designer that is slow in making decisions and is holding up the work process

The first supervisor spends his or her time blaming others for project time and cost problems. When he or she speaks about these problems, it is in terms of "them" or "they" for project overruns or problems. Everything out of his or her mouth seems to be negative.

The second supervisor is subjected to the same problems. However, he or she uses creativity to minimize the impact of the problems. The supervisor uses schedule floats to reduce the impact of the weather and shows the subcontractor that if the firm puts more people on the project that the subcontractor and the project will benefit. The supervisor works with the designer in an effort to speed up the designer's decision making. The second supervisor takes a positive approach to problems; he or she speaks in terms of "we" versus "they."

Problems will always occur in construction. Taking a negative approach will never keep problems from occurring nor minimize their impact. Just like there is "no crying in baseball," there should be "no whining in construction."

2. A system for measuring performance

An effective measuring system involves giving a worker a basis of measuring his or her own individual performance. This includes communicating what is expected of him or her, and communicating how he or she is doing relative to the plan. The plan and subsequent performance system should be communicated both at a job level and at an individual worker level. Leaving the worker in the dark as to what is expected of him or her and how the project is progressing and proceeding does not cultivate a positive worker attitude. Consider the case of a coach of a basketball team. What would happen if the coach told three of the players to go to the locker room while he explained the game plan to two others? Clearly this would cause discontent, a divided team, and a less-than-positive attitude for three of the players. Isn't that what a supervisor is doing when he keeps construction workers in the dark?

The residential builder should give thought to sharing information with workers, such as person-hour budgets and expected productivity for specific work tasks, projected project schedules, and project progress. The alternative is to assume that the workers don't care. This negative assumption promotes a we-versus-they attitude that is sure to result in less-than-satisfactory productivity.

Supervisors *and* their workers are more productive if they know what is expected of them in regard to production, quality, and safety. The construction foremen and his or her crew often go to work and are told what to do without a goal or budget. Having a production goal enables an individual to take pride and satisfaction in meeting that goal. Without a goal, an individual has no system by which to measure his or her effort.

The gap between estimating and construction in many residential building firms has resulted in an estimate not being broken down into daily production goals. During the preplanning phase of the construction process, the estimate should be broken down into daily or hourly production goals for the supervisor. The supervisor should be part of the team that makes these calculations so that he or she can agree to the production goals and become aware of what is expected. As simple a thought as this is, many residential builders and supervisors do not do this; instead, the supervisor is simply assigned to the project and told to construct it. He or she is expected to do the best they can. Goal setting and production goals can go a long way toward increasing productivity and giving the supervisors and crewmembers work satisfaction.

The estimate that is prepared for purposes of bidding the project should be broken down into daily (perhaps hourly) production goals for the supervisor and his or her crew. Supervisors and crewmembers think more in terms of units of work placed per time period rather than units placed per person-hour (i.e. productivity). The transformation of the estimate into daily production goals is made somewhat confusing by the fact that estimates and productivity are often typically expressed in units of work per person-hour as opposed to work per crew hour or time period. Most construction tasks are performed by crews made up of more than one worker.

The transformation of the estimate into daily production goals is not complicated; it merely involves taking the time to do it. It should be done as part of the preplanning process. The determining of production goals from the estimate is illustrated in example below.

The estimate for a project is often prepared and summarized on an estimating form similar to that shown in Figure 2-1.

As an example of preparing production goals for specific work tasks, let us focus on the work task "frame stud walls." The estimator has estimated the following:

FIGURE 2-1 Sample Estimating Form

Work task	Uvs	Quan- tity	Labor productivity	Labor hours	Labor dollars	$/unit of material	Material dollars	Total dollars
Frame stud walls	MBF	10	20 mh/mbf	200	$6,000	$600/mbf	$6,000	$12,000
Frame beams etc. etc.	MBF	5	30 mh/mbf	150	$4,500	$800/sfca	$4,000	$8,500

*Where mbf is an abbreviation for one thousand board feet and sfca is an abbreviation for square feet of contact area.

Quantity of work = 10 MBF
Estimated labor productivity = 20 person-hours per MBF

Therefore the craft hours are estimated as follows:

(10 MBF) ✕ (20 mh/MBF) = 200 craft hours

The production rate the estimator has used (20 mh/MBF) is actually the reciprocal of productivity in that productivity is expressed in units of work per craft-hour. The 20 mh/MBF is equivalent to 0.05 MBF of contact hour per craft-hour. Many estimators prefer to think in terms of craft-hours per unit rather than units per craft-hour.

The production rate of 20 mh/MBF (or productivity of 0.05 MBF craft hours) comes from the estimators' best estimate or forecast of productivity based on past history of doing previous projects. Published cost books such as *R.S. Means* can also be used as guides in estimating the productivity. It is an estimate.

The labor cost estimate or budget is estimated as follows:
(200 craft hours) ✕ (labor rate) =
Assuming an average labor rate of $30.00 per hour:
(200 craft hours) ✕ ($30.00) = $6,000.00

This information above is the format of most construction estimates. It should be broken down into crew or worker production goals per day or per hour. To determine production goals, one of two pieces of information is needed: how long the supervisor has to do the work (activity duration in days) or the size of the work crew(s). One determines the other.

More often than not, the residential builder and supervisor either knows or is given the duration for the work and therefore must determine the crew size to do the work. Let us assume that the "frame stud walls" has to be done in three construction days so that other work can proceed as scheduled. It follows that the supervisor must do 3.33 MBF per day:

A. Calculate needed production per day

Quantity of work to perform	10 MBF
Divided by number of work days	3 days
Equals	3.33 MBF/day

While the number of workers on a crew can vary, the residential builder typically knows the best size crew to use. Work rules (union) may also dictate the composition of the crew; e.g. one laborer for every two carpenters. Let us assume the residential builder plans on using a three-person crew to do the work. Therefore, every crew hour will result in three craft-hours of work. To determine the number of crews that will be required, the estimated productivity and the MBF/day need to be considered.

In the estimate, a production rate of 20 person-hours per MBF was assumed. This is equivalent to a productivity of 0.05 MBF per person hour. It follows that using a three-person crew the MBF placed per day is estimated as follows:

B. Calculate production rate performed per crew-hour

$$\frac{(3 \text{ craft-hours})}{(\text{crew-hour})} \times \frac{(0.05 \text{ MBF})}{(\text{craft-hour})} = \frac{(0.15 \text{ MBF})}{(\text{crew-hour})}$$

Assuming an eight-hour day, one crew is estimated to place the following sfca per day:

C. Calculate production performed by the crew per day

$$\frac{(8 \text{ crew-hours})}{(\text{day})} \times \frac{(0.15 \text{ MBF})}{(\text{crew-hour})} = \frac{(1.20 \text{ MBF})}{(\text{day})}$$

It follows that if the planned duration is such that the work must be done in three days, which can only be accomplished if 3.33 MBF per day, three crews will be needed.

D. Calculate number of crews required

$$\frac{(3.33 \text{ MBF})}{(\text{day})} \div \frac{(1.33 \text{ sfca})}{(\text{MBF per crew})} = 3 \text{ crews}$$

If the residential builder or supervisor cannot use five crews, the supervisor has to consider one of the following:

- Have the smaller number of crews work overtime
- Increase productivity over the 0.05 MBF per person-hour estimated
- Take longer than the planned 3.33 days to do the work

It should be noted that the above calculations assume that the 10 planned workdays are all available. Should the supervisor estimate that on average there is one day of rain for every 3.3 workdays, then the production rate of 0.05 MBF per person-hour and three crews will fall short of getting the work done in 3 days. A larger number of crews, overtime, or a higher production rate would be needed, given one day of rain.

The point is that these production calculations for the crew should be made from the estimate prior to starting the work, during the preplanning phase of the project.

In the above calculations, a crew production rate of 1.2 MBF per day was determined. The supervisor (and his or her crew) should know this production rate so that they have a goal and know what is expected of them. As soon as the crew production rate falls below this 1.2 MBF per day, the supervisor should identify the cause of the problem and implement actions to achieve the 1.2 MBF per day. If the supervisor waits until the third day to see if the planned progress was met, it will be too late to address the productivity problem.

Production goal setting for the crew and workers enables the supervisor to plan and monitor the process rather than attempting to solve the problem when it is too late.

Preplanning crew and craft production rates takes time. However, the supervisor cannot afford not to take the time to plan. The above calculations yielded the following information that is critical to the supervision plan:

Number of crews needed   = 3
Crew production rate per day = 1.2 MBF/hour

Ideally, each and every work task that is estimated in the bidding phase is broken down into production goals for the construction phase. At the very minimum, key or "vital few" work tasks are broken down into production goals.

3. An effective communication channel

Poor communication at jobsites leads to unnecessary redo work, poor worker attitudes, and an inability to properly monitor work progress. There are two types of communication that are critical to a productive jobsite: oral communication and written communication.

Effective and productive communication at a jobsite is complicated by the fact that communications are carried out in the open during a relatively noisy job process, and by the fact that the individuals may have different vocabularies and different communication skills. A construction craftsman, foreman, superintendent, project manager, and architect may all speak and interpret various phrases and words differently.

Effective communication entails listening as well as talking. All too often the contractor supervisor only talks at the worker instead of asking the worker for ideas and listening to his or her concerns. On occasion, the person who knows how to form the concrete or place rebar may be the craftsman, not the supervisor. Failure to take advantage of the workers' knowledge could mean missing out on an improved construction method and may adversely affect the attitude of the craftsman. If a worker knows a better way to do something but is not being asked for his or her ideas, he or she could develop an "I don't care" attitude.

Effective supervisor communications also entails taking the time to properly explain the work process to the worker. The construction craftsman may think he or she is supposed to know how to do something even if he or she doesn't. Confused as to what to do, rather than ask for an explanation, the worker may proceed to do the work incorrectly. The end result is that the residential builder will have to correct the work later—a non-productive work process.

The construction industry has been characterized for many years as an industry with inadequate written communications at the jobsite. Inaccurate time cards, late reports, failure to give the worker or supervisor written feedback, and lost or misplaced documents are typical of the construction jobsite. Part of the reason for written-communication inadequacies relates to the decentralized nature of the work process. Unlike most industries, which create and monitor their written communication system at the same place they make their product, in the construction industry, written communication is often created at the jobsite, transferred to the contractor's main office, and hopefully communicated back to the jobsite. This process results in untimely and sometimes incorrect reports.

The supervisor often complains about bad record keeping they get at the jobsite; but, in fact, he himself may promote bad record keeping. For example, a weekly timecard that requires the foreman to keep track of workers' hours charged to specific work tasks is likely to be filled out weekly rather than daily. The result is that the foreman cannot remember on Friday what the workers did on Monday. Perhaps a daily timecard preprinted with work codes would ensure more accurate data and improve proper charging of labor hours. In addition, the use of daily report forms that require supervisors merely to check items like the weather conditions rather than describe them is more likely to be legible and to lessen the time needed for the recording process.

In critiquing their own written communication process or system, the contractor should remember the following three rules for improving the accuracy and timeline of the jobsite record-keeping process.

1. An individual that is required to fill out a form should be shown where the data goes and how it is used.

2. An individual that is required to fill out a form should be shown by example that their data was in fact used.
3. Any individual that fills out a form or inputs data should be given a subsequent feedback report or data.

Given these rules, the firm should consider posting, at a very visible worker location, a flowchart of the information system being used at the jobsite. Also consider posting a sign or report that charts project progress against planned progress, which will help workers measure their progress, improve communications, and aid in making the job look like a firm. In summary, the supervisor should work at improving the oral and written communication process at the jobsite with a twofold objective: to produce more timely and accurate data and reports, and to use the communication process to get all the jobsite personnel aligned to the company's project goals.

4. Monetary benefits

Some would suggest that workers are only in it for the money. If that is the case, why do workers take days off with no pay? Or why do workers that have attained sufficient wealth continue to work? Yes, money is important, but it is not the only need of workers. Pride, a measuring system, and a communication channel also are important needs.

Some of the classical studies on why workers produce indicate that money or financial gain is only one of several worker needs. For example, in Mazlow's theory on work, he defines five worker needs. In this theory, workers initially work to gain financial security and to purchase needed assets such as a home and personal belongings. However, once a worker achieves these needs, then he or she can only be motivated by what Mazlow refers to as "inner needs," which include responsibility, communication, and pride[1]. Similarly, in Herzberg's study of workers, he devised a model referred to as the Motivational-Maintenance model. Money is defined as a maintenance factor or need. In this theory, if the maintenance factor (money) is taken away from a worker, it will dismotivate the worker and negatively impact productivity. On the other hand, it is not a motivational factor, which means giving more of it will not likely result in more productivity[2].

In all likelihood, it follows that every worker is different. Some are driven by the need for money and security, others are driven by pride, and still others are driven by measurement data or the ability to communicate. Therefore, it is important that the residential builder and the supervisor recognize what motivates and what does not motivate each and every worker. No two workers are likely the same when it comes to what motivates them.

Group Behavior

Much of the behavior of the individual employee can be understood only in the context of the group in which he or she works. Commitment to production goals, acceptance of leadership, satisfaction with work, and effectiveness of performance all tend to depend on the relations of a person with his or her co-workers. The effects of group behavior and the work environment on the individual worker are especially important with regard to construction productivity and personnel management.

Very little construction work is done by an individual in isolation. Instead, several laborers representing more than one type of craft interact in the building process. Labor unions often require that several types of craftspeople work together. For example, many union agreements require the use of a laborer to help two carpenters. Even if individuals are not mixed together for a particular type of work, they still interact with fellow workers during lunch or non-work hours. As time goes on, groups of workers begin to share common goals and values.

From a sociological point of view, a group is more than just a collection of individuals working together in one location. A group is formed only as a result of interpersonal relations. Researchers describe the process of group formation as the result of the following four essential characteristics:

1. A motivational base shared by individuals and conducive to recurrent interaction among them.
2. An organization (group structure) consisting of roles differentiated in some degree from those of nonmembers.

3. A shared set of norms (values, rules, and standards of behavior).
4. More or less consistent effects, produced by the group, on the attitudes and behavior of individual members.

A construction union, which includes all construction labor in a given craft, is itself a group. It has traits that are similar to the four characteristics just listed. Smaller groups of individuals within a union and employed at a particular project site also share these characteristics.

Groups are often classified by type. Groups are classified as either formal or informal. Examples of formal groups include business organizations and professional associations; informal groups result from when individuals with common social interests come together. Although formal groups influence individual workers with their policies, informal groups are often more difficult to control and as such have a greater influence on personnel management. Informal groups result when individuals with common social interests come together and can be further classified as one of the following three types:

1. Large groups that arise because of internal politics. These types of groups often are referred to as "gangs" or "crowds."
2. Groups formed on the basis of common jobs. Members are often intimate and work, talk, and even dine together. This type of group often is referred to as a "clique."
3. Small groups consisting of two or three close friends. This type of group often is referred to as a "sub-clique."

Each of these three types of informal groups can be observed in the construction industry. Union workers gathering for a labor strike or forming a group to protest nonunion work can be classified as a gang or crowd. Cliques are common on a construction project. Often several workers may share a sport or hobby that brings them together. Cliques can prove beneficial or detrimental to productivity, depending on their goals and values. Smaller groups of two or three workers who live close to one another are typically friends who share common interests and may prefer to work together. Generally, this type of group presents few problems with regard to personnel management.

Firms can do little, however, to prevent the formation of cliques, and nothing a firm does will permanently destroy this type of group. One of the results of the now widely recognized study at the Hawthorne plant of Western Electric was to confirm the existence and importance of such informal groups. The Hawthorne study analyzed that cliques were a significant part of the organization. Employees had social needs that they sought to satisfy at work. This fact resulted in a system of cliques, rivalries, and grapevines, all of which influenced employee behavior[3].

Even if a firm can prevent the existence of cliques, doing so may not be advantageous. If the goals of the clique are consistent with those of the firm, the firm will reap the benefits; however, a clique may prove to be a productivity constraint if its goals or values differ from those of the firm. With proper leadership, the goals and values of the clique and the firm can be made compatible.

It is the residential builder's and supervisor's duty to encourage meaningful group goals. Without them, group members are unlikely to share common work objectives. If group goals are vague and workers interpret them differently, the possibility of increased productivity is lessened. The supervisor must also see that workers in a group understand the relations between their personal objectives and group goals. Group values favoring higher productivity are likely to develop when workers understand group goals, understand how their own objectives relate to those of their group or clique, and find meaning and satisfaction in the work they do.

3

Practical Planning and Scheduling

Project planning and scheduling involves preparing a formal "road map" of how the overall project will be undertaken. A project is broken down into a series of activities by the project planner and sequenced to show the relationships of the various activities. Work durations are assigned to each activity to determine the overall project duration.

There are several planning and scheduling procedures or algorithms available to the residential builder, including a bar chart and various network techniques such as critical path method (CPM). However, formal procedures have not been widely used in the construction industry. Historically, residential builders have carried project plans "in their heads," not taking the time to prepare rigorous plans and schedules. There is considerable evidence that the failure to do so weighs negatively on the firm. Excessive jobsite waiting time, duplication of incorrectly placed work, and nonproductive time resulting from unnecessary labor, equipment, or material transportation all stem in part from the lack of thorough project planning and scheduling.

Partly as a result of the increased use of computers in the construction industry and partly because of pressures placed on the residential builder by the customer or project owner, firms have been increasing their use of plans and schedules. Most firms that prepare them use them to set activity milestone dates and to establish the duration of an entire project. Yet a plan and schedule also can be a means of optimally utilizing project resources, including labor.

After presenting the basis of formal planning and scheduling techniques—CPM—this chapter focuses on using plans and schedules to optimize jobsite productivity. Several planning and scheduling techniques will be illustrated.

What is Project Planning and Scheduling?

A formal project plan and schedule includes the following elements:

- Breakdown of a project into a series of individual "work pieces"
- Determination of work piece durations and required crews
- Sequencing of work pieces in an overall project plan
- Calculation of project duration as a function of work piece durations and sequencing
- Determination of activity "float times" or possible delay times available to a manager to use during unexpected and uncontrollable events

Two of the more widely used planning and scheduling techniques for construction projects are the bar chart and CPM. The use of these techniques often results in a graphical presentation of a small project such as that shown in Figure 3-1.

Figure 3-1 is referred to as a bar chart. For more complex projects there may be many more work pieces or activities than those shown in the figure. Nonetheless, the principles of preparing a plan and schedule remain essentially unchanged.

Why Undertake Project Planning and Scheduling?

One of the most prevalent and detrimental reasons for low industry productivity is the lack of project planning and scheduling. Failure to plan or schedule activities leads to excessive labor and equipment waiting time, delays related to unavailability of materials, lack of subcontractor coordination, and management's inability to react to unexpected events such as poor weather, equipment breakdowns, or material shortages.

A residential builder would not bid or start a project without first preparing an on-paper, detailed cost estimate-in effect, a plan for

FIGURE 3-1 Example of a "Simple" Project Plan

Activity	Start	Finish	Sept. 4-8	Sept. 11-15	Sept. 18-22	Sept. 25-29	Oct. 2-6	Oct. 9-13	Oct. 16-20
Excavate	Sept. 1	Sept. 13							
Obtain Sub-base	Sept. 1	Sept. 26							
Obtain Pipe	Sept. 1	Sept. 26							
Place Pipe	Sept. 27	Sept. 29							
Fine Grade	Sept. 29	Oct. 6							
Place Sub-base	Oct. 6	Oct. 10							
Compact Sub-base	Oct. 10	Oct. 13							
Place Concrete	Oct. 13	Oct. 17							
Excess Sub-base	Oct. 17	Oct. 23							
Backfill	Oct. 20	Oct. 29							

costs. However, the same firm will often ignore the need to prepare an on-paper plan and schedule. Instead, the firm might argue that a formal plan is subject to too much uncertainty. In reality, the very existence of a plan and schedule can enable a project manager, superintendent, or foreman to effectively react to the many uncertain, unexpected events that characterize the construction process. The more uncertain the production process, the stronger the need to prepare and use a plan and schedule.

The relationship of formal project planning and scheduling and productivity is illustrated in Figures 3-2 and 3-3. Figure 3-2 summarizes the findings of an industrial engineering-based study performed at a project (on a sample day). The figure indicates that direct work was being performed only 42 percent of the time. Undoubtedly, some projects do much better in regard to this percentage of productive work—but some are worse.

As Figures 3-2 shows, all jobs include a significant percentage of waiting time, unnecessary traveling time, and time related to redoing

FIGURE 3-2 Possible Impact of Poor Planning and Scheduling

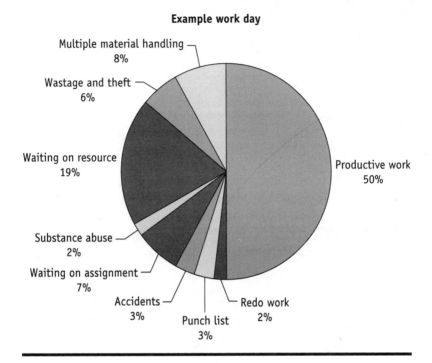

Example work day

Multiple material handling
8%

Wastage and theft
6%

Waiting on resource
19%

Productive work
50%

Substance abuse
2%

Waiting on assignment
7%

Accidents
3%

Punch list
3%

Redo work
2%

work or to poor communication. These time components of an eight-hour day are all nonproductive. They take away from the profit objectives of the residential builder, lead to negative work attitudes, and have a significant negative impact on productivity.

A plan and schedule that sets out material procurement dates will help reduce delays and waiting time associated with material shortages. Similarly, a plan for labor and subcontractor performance can result in a more productive use of available labor crafts and increase subcontractor coordination, attitude, and productivity.

Another way of quantifying the relationship of project planning and scheduling and productivity is illustrated in Figure 3-3. This figure plots a bar-chart type of schedule for a small project that consists of 10 work activities. If the activity is to be performed effectively, each of these activities requires a finite number of resources. Assume we know optimal crew sizes and have designated the crew-size num-

FIGURE 3-3 Example of Planned Nonproductive Time

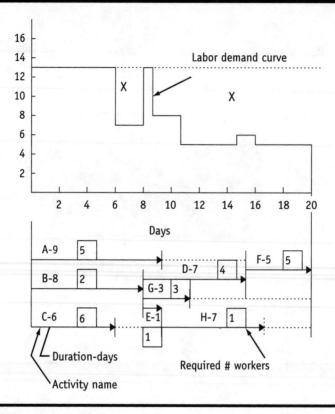

ber inside the block beside the activity to which each corresponds. We also have plotted the number of laborers needed on any one day-a maximum of 13. (The actual number needed on any one day varies significantly from one to the next.)

It is unlikely that the residential builder can hire and fire laborers (or any other resource) on a daily basis according to the labor demand curve shown in the figure. Instead, the residential builder probably has a non-optimal number of laborers at the jobsite on any given day. For example, assume that the firm keeps 13 laborers at the site every day for the project's duration. This is illustrated by the horizontal line (solid and dashed) at 13 laborers. The areas marked "X" represent "planned nonproductive time" a laborer is actually scheduled to be nonproductive.

If a superintendent has five person-days of work scheduled on a given day and has 10 workers there to perform the work, the 10 workers will produce five person-days of work; that is, they will be 50 percent productive. The challenge of the planning and scheduling effort thus becomes evident. Until a project plan and schedule can be prepared that results in a daily matching of availability and demand for project resources, there will be "planned" nonproductive time.

Implementing a Project Plan and Schedule

A project plan and schedule should be a means of integrating all the entities of a project into an overall team: the firm's project manager, superintendent, foremen, and subcontractors. The plan and schedule fail as the weakest link.

The difficulty of preparing a plan and schedule is compounded by the organizational structure of the residential project. For example, an in-the-office project manager may have the responsibility for putting together a plan and schedule before the contractor even assigns a specific superintendent or foreman to the project. Even after they are selected, a few of them may be negligent in providing input to the scheduling effort, which can weaken it.

The following are guidelines for the preferred timing of each step of the planning process:

1. The project manager prepares a "milestone" or conceptual schedule prior to the project bid as a basis for proceeding with the project estimate.
2. With input from field personnel, including the superintendent, and from potential subcontractors, the residential builder's project manager prepares a detailed plan and schedule as part of the cost estimate/bid.
3. Upon being awarded the contract, the residential builder forces subcontractor input and makes any necessary scheduling modifications.
4. The detailed project plan and schedule is communicated to all field personnel, including the superintendent, foremen, and subcontractors.
5. Daily, field personnel are required to make use of the plan and schedule, including performing "short interval scheduling" (described in later sections).

6. Weekly, job progress should be documented and incorporated into the plan and schedule.
7. Weekly, with the help of all field personnel, the plan and schedule is revised. Management decisions and preferred actions are determined, and should be implemented by the superintendent, foremen, and subcontractors with the objective of controlling project time and cost.

Steps in Preparing and Using a Detailed Plan and Schedule

1. Defining work activities

The first step in preparing a formal plan and schedule is to define the project work pieces or activities. For example, should "form concrete slab," "place rebar in the slab," and "pour concrete in the slab" be defined as three activities or as one activity, "place slabs"? At what level of detail should activities be defined? This is a more critical issue than one might think. Too detailed a list of activities will frustrate jobsite personnel, whereas too few activities will result in the schedule being of little help as a productivity or control tool. This much can be said: a broader list of activities needs to be defined for a milestone or conceptual schedule than for the detailed schedule that will be used at the jobsite.

While it is impossible to set out a specific "best" list of activities for each project, one can establish the following criteria for defining project activities:

- The activities should be compatible with the intended purpose and use of the schedule.
- To the degree feasible, the activities should be compatible with the estimate breakdown.
- The activities should be compatible with field reporting for cost control.
- The activities should be compatible with the firm's billing system used for making progress pay requests.
- Any work function that requires a unique set of resources should be defined as a unique work activity.

More often than not, the use of these criteria will result in the residential builder defining between 30 and 100 work activities for the detailed schedule. The actual number will depend on the project size, work complexity, the ability to revise the schedule periodically, and the ability of onsite personnel to use the schedule information.

2. *Determining activity durations*

There is only one accurate and acceptable way to determine activity durations. The duration of every activity must be determined on the basis of the quantity of work, the crew to be assigned to the work activity, and the estimate of the crew's productivity. Like cost estimating, determining activity durations is subject to uncertainty and contains a degree of risk.

The following is one example of determining activity duration. In this instance, the activity is erecting forms.

1. Determine quantity of work   8,000 sfca
2. Estimate productivity   10 mh/100 sfca
3. Establish crew size   5 workers
4. Calculate duration:

$$\frac{(10\text{mh})\ (8{,}000\ \text{sfca})}{(100\text{sfca})(5\text{mh/r})(8\ \text{hr/day})} = 20\ \text{days}$$

The above calculation needs to be performed for each work activity for the project schedule. A form for making these calculations is shown in Figure 3-4. If an activity is to be subcontracted, the duration should be estimated or determined from subcontractor input.

3. *Determining activity sequencing or logic*

Project work activities must be sequenced to reflect the actual planned progress of the residential project. This sequencing reflects the technology of construction-it is technically impossible to do certain construction operations or activities until certain other tasks are performed. If a project plan and schedule are to be properly prepared, they must reflect three types of logic sequencing:

FIGURE 3-4 Form for Determining Activity Duration

Job Name: _____

Activity: _____

Date: _____

Planner: _____

1. Quantity of work to be performed:_____

2. Possible crew sizes:

    Type of crew & # of workers   **Productivity (units/crew hr)**

    _____   _____

    _____   _____

    _____   _____

3. Crew selected _____

4. Activity duration:

    Hours = Quantity work / Crew productivity = _____

    Days = Hours / Hours per day (8)   = _____

---

1. Technical logic (based on the technology of construction)
2. Resource logic (based on availability of resources)
3. Preference logic (which recognizes project economics)

Technical logic relates to the fact that certain construction work activities cannot get started until a prior work activity is done; for example you cannot put up sheathing until the studs are placed. Resource logic addresses the fact that although it may be possible to perform two work activities at the same time (such as forming the north and east slabs), because of limited resources (say, carpenters) it may not be possible to undertake the two activities together. Preference logic addresses the fact that despite technical ability and the availability of resources, the residential builder may decide for economic reasons to do one activity after another.

4. Adjusting activity durations for contingencies

In an environment of uncertainty (such as poor weather, material shortages, equipment breakdowns), it is unrealistic for a contractor to plan for ideal activity durations. Once the activity sequencing is determined and the project plan is sketched, the preparer of the detailed plan and schedule may decide that it is necessary to make some activity duration adjustments. For example, the initial sketch may indicate that certain concrete work will be performed during months when several rainy days are expected; seeing this, the preparer may want to add a day or two to the duration of the concrete work. A plan that does not include such contingencies is unrealistic, misleading, and may prove detrimental to management decisions.

5. Obtaining subcontractor input

Construction of a residential unit entails the coordination of many interdependent contractors. The supervisor must obtain timely and accurate subcontractor information, including input from specialty contractors. On occasion, this becomes a difficult task. The best way to obtain subcontractor schedule input is to require it contractually. If the subcontractor fails to cooperate, he or she can be penalized: the retainer can be held or he or she can simply not be rehired. A contractual requirement that the subcontractor submit a weekly form, such as that shown in Figure 3-5, can be used to ensure that this input is provided. Showing the subcontractor how his or her timely and accurate schedule information can prevent problems and increase productivity will help to encourage the subcontractor's cooperation.

6. Drawing the project schedule

Once activities have been defined, durations determined, and the sequencing of the activities determined, the project plan can be drawn. This can be done using a bar graph or a CPM diagram. Figure 3-1 is a sample bar graph for a small project. The activities are shown as bars: the beginning of the bar designates the start of the activity and the end of the bar shows the planned completion of the activity. The actual progress of the project is often superimposed on the bar chart alongside the planned progress.

FIGURE 3-5 Form for Obtaining Subcontractor Input

Activities required to complete your work	Code or letter for work activity	Estimated duration	Activity must follow activities (list codes)

Sketch work plan below via an activity arrow diagram

|———————————|————————————|————————————|———————————|

There are several different formats in which to draw the CPM diagram, three of which are shown in Figures 3-6, 3-7, and 3-8. Figure 3-6 uses arrows to represent work activities. Specific planned milestone dates can be set in the circles at the end of the arrows. These milestone dates can be interim progress dates specified by contract or by the project planner.

The second CPM option, shown in Figure 3-7, is commonly referred to as a "circle notation" CPM diagram or a "precedence" diagram. In it, work activities are represented by individual circles. The arrows between the circles are used to specify the sequencing or logic of the activities.

In the third CPM diagram, shown in Figure 3-8, the individual activity arrows are proportional in length to the activity durations. This CPM diagram, perhaps the most useful as a visual tool, is commonly referred to as a "time scale" CPM diagram. The dashed lines following the activity arrows represent activity "float" or slack times during which a manager can react to uncertain

FIGURE 3-6 Arrow Notation CPM

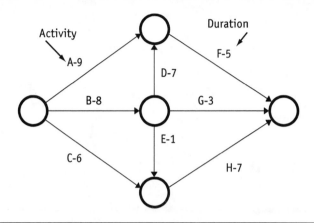

events. An explanation of the calculation of activity float or slack time follows.

Thus, there are several different means by which the residential builder may draw the overall project plan and schedule. Whatever way is chosen, it is important that the plan and schedule be drawn in a manner that is easily understood by field personnel.

7. *Performing CPM calculations*

Although the establishment of project goals is the major benefit of a project plan and schedule, other benefits can be derived. In

FIGURE 3-7 Circle Notation or Precedence CPM

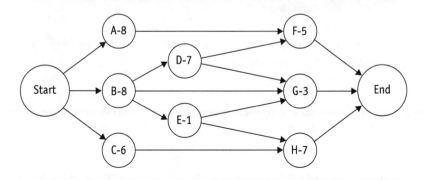

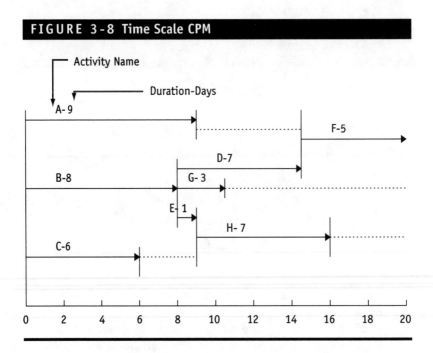

FIGURE 3-8 Time Scale CPM

particular, if the CPM technique is utilized, calculations can be performed to determine a project's duration, the so-called critical path of its activities, and the float or slack time, which is the management time available for all work activities. These types of information might be referred to as the three objectives of basic CPM calculations. The calculations can be performed efficiently with a computer, but their simplicity makes it possible to perform them without one. Even if a computer is available, knowing how to make the CPM calculations manually enhances the understanding and use of the CPM process.

We can illustrate CPM calculations using the simple CPM diagrams shown in Figure 3-6, 3-7, or 3-8, but will focus on Figure 3-6. The planned duration of each CPM activity is placed beside the corresponding activity. In the CPM diagram shown in Figure 3-6, there is no intended relation between the length of an arrow representing an activity and the duration of the activity.

CPM calculations are made by means of a forward and a backward pass of calculations through the diagram. The forward pass is referred to as the latest-start-time schedule. In performing the two sets of calculations we will generate five different types of information for each activity:

1. Earliest start time for an activity (EST)
2. Earliest finish time for an activity (EFT)
3. Latest start time for an activity (LST)
4. Latest finish time for an activity (LFT)
5. Total float time of an activity (TF)

The EST for an activity is defined as the earliest possible time at which the activity can start. Assuming a start date for the project as the end of day 0 (equivalent to the beginning of day 1), the earliest start times of activities A, B, and C are 0. (CPM activity durations can be given in hours, days, or weeks; also, by using a calendar we can make calendar-day calculations rather than working-day calculations) The EST answers along with answers to the other calculations are given in Figure 3-9.

The EFT of an activity is defined and calculated as an activity's earliest start time plus the activity's duration. In other words, if activity A can start on the end of day 0 and takes nine days to complete, the soonest A can be completed is the end of day 9.

The EST of any given activity is calculated as the maximum EFTs of activities immediately preceding it. In the case of activity D, only one activity, B, directly precedes it. Therefore, the EST of activity D is equal to the EFT of activity B, or the end of the eighth day.

FIGURE 3-9 CPM Calculations

Activity	Duration	EST	EFT	LST	LFT	TF
A	9	0	9	6	15	6
B	8	0	8	0	8	0
C	6	0	6	7	13	7
D	7	8	15	8	15	0
E	1	8	9	12	13	4
F	5	15	20	15	20	0
G	3	8	11	17	20	9
H	7	9	16	13	20	4

Other activity ESTs and EFTs can be calculated in a similar manner. Consider activity F, shown in Figure 3-6. Its start is constrained by activities A and D. The EFTs of activities A and D are 9 and 15, respectively. Because activity F cannot start until both activity A and D are complete, activity F's EST is the larger of the two EFTs, or 15. The ESTs and EFTs of all the activities shown in Figure 3-6 are given in Figure 3-9.

Because activities F, G, and H terminate the project, the largest EFT of these three activities is the minimum project completion date. The EFTs of activities F, G, and H are 20, 11, and 16, respectively; therefore, the minimum project completion time is 20 days.

The LST and LFT for each activity are calculated from a backward pass through the CPM network. As a starting point for the calculations, the project duration is set equal to the minimum project duration (20 days in the example in Figure 3-6 and Figure 3-9). The LFT of an activity is defined as the latest possible time at which an activity can finish without delaying the predetermined project completion date. Because activities F, G, and H are terminating activities in the CPM diagram, their LFTs are 20 (see Figure 3-9).

The LST of an activity is the activity's LFT minus the activity's duration. Because activity F has a duration of five days and must be completed by the end of the twentieth day, it must be started no later than the end of the fifteenth day (20 - 5 = 15).

The LFT of a given activity is equal to the minimum LST of the activities immediately following it. Therefore, the LFTs of activities A and D are 15 (the LST of activity F).

The LSTs and LFTs of the remaining activities shown in Figure 3-9 are calculated in a similar manner. Activity B, for instance, has three activities immediately following it. Thus, activity B's LFT is the smallest of the LSTs of activities D, E, or G, which are 8, 12, or 17, respectively. The LFT of activity B therefore is 8.

The last CPM calculation involves determining each activity's total float time, which is the amount of time for which an activity can be delayed, assuming no other activity is delayed, without affecting the minimum completion date of the project. Total float time is a function of the earliest and latest start times.

Total float time for an activity is the difference between the LST and the EST for an activity. It also can be determined by taking the difference between an activity's LFT and EFT. Either of these calculations will yield the same total float value. The calculated total float times for the activities are given in Figure 3-9 for the CPM diagram shown in Figure 3-6. Activities B, D, and F have total float times of 0. The LSTs and ESTs for these activities are equal, as are their LFTs and EFTs. In other words, these activities cannot be delayed. They dictate the minimum project duration and form a critical path through the CPM network. The second basic CPM objective is thus complete, and the critical path is indicated by the activities that have the least amount of total float time (in this case, 0).

Our third objective, that of determining possible float times for the activities, also is complete. The total float times given in the table show the amount of possible time each of the noncritical activities can be delayed without affecting the project completion date.

8. *Undertaking short-interval scheduling*

The planning and scheduling discussed to this point pertains to the project at large. However, there is another level of planning and scheduling that should take place and can yield equal productivity benefits. This level of planning—short-interval scheduling-requires planning tomorrow's work today.

All too often the project superintendent or foreman reacts to problems at the site rather than taking earlier steps to prevent the problems from occurring. As much as 10 percent of the day at a jobsite is nonproductive because of the need to look for tools or equipment while a craftsperson or entire crew is waiting for them. Not planning tomorrow's work today leads to numerous unnecessary double lifting and movement of materials.

A simple form such as the one shown in Figure 3-10, if used on a daily basis by the superintendent or foreman in conjunction with the overall project plan and schedule, has the potential to increase job productivity by 10 percent or more. The form requires that the superintendent or foreman do the following daily (near the end of the day):

FIGURE 3-10 Form for Short Interval Scheduling

Job Name: _____

Date: _____

Day of week: _____

Supervisor: _____

Type of work planned for tomorrow	Quantity of work to be achieved	Resources needed: tools, equipment, material, workers
1. _____	_____	_____
2. _____	_____	_____
3. _____	_____	_____
4. _____	_____	_____
5. _____	_____	_____

---

1. Set out the type of work to be performed the next day
2. Set out a quantity goal to be achieved the next day
3. Set out the tools, equipment, and resources, including labor that will be needed to achieve the work goal

9. Using the CPM results

The CPM process can yield benefits over and above the three basic objectives of establishing the latest project completion date, the critical path, and the float or slack times for all activities. Several of the extended benefits, including cash management, good billing and pay request procedures, and proper allocation of resources (such as labor) to the project, are best obtained using a computer and accompanying software. Even without a computer, however, relatively simple but practical benefits can be obtained if the project planner is aware of float times. Consider the CPM diagram shown in Figure 3-8. It is a time scale schedule for the arrow notation CPM diagram in Figure 3-6. Suppose that it rains an unexpected amount on day two and three and that activities A, B, and C cannot proceed if it rains. Assume further that in preparing the construction plan and schedule, the construction planner did not anticipate rain. The obvious question is whether the project will take more than 20 days or units of time. At first glance, it may seem so, because of activity B, which is on the critical path, has been delayed two days. However, activities A and C have total float times of six and four days, respectively. Therefore, it may be possible to take resources from these two activities on days 4, 5, and 6 if necessary and assign them to activity B to enable it to catch up to its original eight-day duration and maintain a 20-day schedule.

This example is a simple but practical application of the CPM technique. Other practical applications of the concept of float times include using them to prepare a schedule that better utilizes resources from the point of view of productivity. Figure 3-3 adds a resource requirement (number of laborers required) to each of the activities in Figure 3-8 and also shows the cumulative number of laborers needed on any one day to complete the schedule as shown (the earliest-start-time schedule).

Earlier, we characterized this schedule as one that required residential builders to hire and fire as needed or to hire more laborers than needed on several days. Neither alternative is preferred. Can a better schedule be prepared for the 20-day project that satisfies the technical, resource, and preference logic and makes more productive use of assigned laborers? The answer is yes. It is possible to shift activities within their float times to yield the schedule illustrated in Figure 3-11. This schedule requires only 10 laborers, not the 13 previously required (a 30 percent decrease). The schedule makes better use of assigned laborers and results in a better matching of availability and demand for resources as well as improved productivity.

By using the floats that were calculated in Figure 3-9, the scheduler can resequence activities to level the number of workers needed on any specific day. This is just one of the many applications of using floats to perform resource management. There are many algorithms that can be used to schedule resources to meet a specific objective. The point is that the floats that were calculated in Figure 3-9 represent available time for the scheduler

FIGURE 3-11 Time Scale CPM

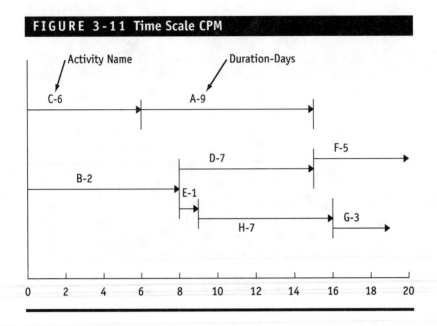

to meet specific objectives, be it leveling resources, recovering lost project time, or another defined objective.

10. Updating a project plan and schedule

It is critical that the initial project plan and schedule, be it a bar chart or CPM diagram, be updated as the job progresses. If the initial plan and schedule are not updated, they can lead to poor daily management decisions.

When a 10-month project is two months old, one can argue that there is a new eight-month project to be started. The events that have occurred during the first two months of the project should be recognized which may change the critical path, the project duration, or even require adjustments in the duration or crew sizes needed for remaining activities.

Fundamental to updating a schedule to reflect what has happened to date is obtaining timely field data. This requires a commitment to accurate field reporting. The use of a daily report such as that shown in Figure 3-12 can be used for this purpose.

FIGURE 3-12 Form for Updating a Schedule

Activities worked	Percentage	Need to revise	Revised duration	Remarks
1.				
2.				
3.				
4.				
5.				
6.				
7.				
8.				
9.				
10.				

Comments regarding work progress or difficulties: _____

_____

_____

_____

Actual revisions of the project plan and schedule, including revised CPM calculations, are best achieved with a computer; however, even absent of a computer, the need for updating exists, and a project plan and schedule can be updated manually in a simplified form.

4

Implementing an Effective Control System

Controlling project time and cost is key to the residential builder's profitability and the ability to complete a project on time and on budget. While the project estimate and the project schedule set out the potential for profits and an on-time project schedule, it is the control task that enables the contractor to achieve the profit and schedule.

A control system has five key elements:

1. In a *timely* manner
2. it compares *actual*
3. to *plan,*
4. with the objective of *detecting a problem*
5. and a *follow-up action* is taken in an attempt to correct the problem.

If any one of these five elements is absent or done improperly, the control process fails.

Job-control Reporting Process

The objective of the job-control report is to enable the residential builder to "see" the status of an in progress project from the company office. The company owner and his key company personnel, including project managers, cannot be at every job all the time. It is the timely job-control report that provides the firm with the opportunity to see the project from the office.

The largest risk factor, and potentially the largest profit center, for the residential builder is the onsite, self-performed labor cost. Two key jobsite reports support the preparation of the job-control report—the daily report that summarizes quantities in place and the timecard that summarizes craft-hours worked. This process is shown in Figure 4-1.

In order to be effective, the budgeted quantities and craft-hours have to be accurate. Equally important, the field reporting system must be timely and accurate. The source documents for the quantities of work put in place to date and the craft-hours expended to date are the daily reports and the time cards filled out at the jobsite. We will return to the need for accurate and timely data in a later section of this chapter.

Residential builders use various formats of the job-control report. One format is shown in Figure 4-2. This format can hardly be viewed as being effective because it merely measures the labor hours expended to date against the budget. This enables the residential builder to detect a problem when the labor hours exceed the budgeted hours, but much too late to be able to make corrective actions. For example, the report shown in Figure 4-2 would enable the firm to know they have a productivity (and cost overrun) problem with

FIGURE 4-1 Example Columns for a Job-control Report

Take-off items from drawings	Take-off quantities by estimator	Budgeted hours based on historical data	Quantities to date from daily reports at job	Craft-hours to date from daily timecards	Calculated from data in 4 previous columns
Work Item	Budgeted Quantity	Budgeted Hours	Actual Quantity	Actual Hours	Projected Over or Under Hours

FIGURE 4-2 Comparing Actual Hours to Date Versus Budgeted Hours

Name of Work Item	Budgeted Quantity	Budgeted Craft-hours	Budgeted Craft-hours
Form Slabs	500	500	350
Rough Carpentry	200	300	150
Roofing	100	200	80

forming slabs when the actual craft-hours exceeded the budgeted 500 craft-hours.

A more effective control report that monitors percentage of effort or labor hours expended versus the percentage of work put in place is illustrated in Figure 4-3. In Figure 5-3, 500 units of work (forming is usually measured in square feet of contact area) and 500 craft-hours are budgeted. At the time of the job-control report shown, 250 units of work are in place. This represents 50 percent of the budgeted quantity. However, the firm already has expended 350 craft-hours to do the work, which is 70 percent of the budgeted craft-hours.

Looked at another way, it has taken 350 craft-hours to place 50 percent of the quantity of work. If this productivity (man-hours per unit) trend continues, it will take a total of 700 craft-hours to complete all the work-200 more man-hours than budgeted. This 200 man-hour variance is projected in the last column of Figure 4-3.

A similar analysis of comparing the percentage of quantity in place to hours expected to date indicates that the carpentry work item is right on budget. The roofing item is projected to come under budget by 40 craft-hours.

Using the control system report shown in Figure 4-3, the residential builder can detect a potential problem as soon as the percentage of labor hours expended is greater than the percentage of work put in place. This potential problem may occur as soon as the work is barely started. Early detection of a productivity problem is critical to the firm's ability to correct a problem.

Comparing hours, labor costs, or unit costs can make this comparison of the percentage of work put in place versus the percentage

FIGURE 4-3 Job-control Report by Comparing Percentage of Hours to Percentage of Work in Place

Name of Work Item	Budgeted Quantity	Budgeted Hours	Actual Quantity to Date	Percent of Quantity in Place	Actual Hours to Date	Percent of Hours to Date	Variance at Completion
Form Slabs	500	500	250	50	350	70	+200 hrs
Carpentry Framing	200	300	100	50	150	50	—
Roofing	100	200	50	50	80	40	−40 hrs

of effort expended to date. A report illustrating labor dollars instead of labor hours is illustrated in Figure 4-4. An hourly rate of $20 per hour is assumed in Figure 4-4. The variances in the last column are calculated the same way as they were in Figure 4-3. For example, it has taken $7,000 of labor cost to do 50 percent of the work item "Form Slabs." If the productivity stays the same, it will take $14,000 to complete the work-an overrun of $4,000.

A similar report using unit costs is illustrated in Figure 4-5. The $20 unit cost for the work item "Form Slabs" is determined in the estimating process by dividing the $10,000 budget (i.e. 500 craft-hours at $20 per hour), by the budgeted 500 units of work to do. The actual unit cost of $28 for the "Form Slabs" work item at the date of the report is determined by dividing the $7,000 cost to date by the 250 units of work put in place to date. Using this report, any

FIGURE 4-4 Job-control Report by Comparing Percentage of Dollars Expended to Percentage of Work in Place

Name of Work Item	Budgeted Quantity	Budgeted Hours	Actual Quantity to Date	Percent of Quantity in Place	Actual Hours to Date	Percent of Hours to Date	Variance at Completion
Form Slabs	500	$10,000	250	50	$7,000	70	+$4,000
Carpentry Framing	200	$6,000	100	50	$3,000	50	—
Roofing	100	$4,000	50	50	$1,600	40	−$800

FIGURE 4-5 Job-control Report by Comparing Unit Costs

Name of Work Item	Budgeted Quantity	Budgeted Unit Cost	Actual Quantity to Date	Actual Unit Cost to Date	Forecast Variance to Completion
Form Slabs	500	$20.00	250	$28.00	+$4,000
Carpentry					
Framing	200	$30.00	100	$30.00	—
Roofing	100	$40.00	50	$32.00	-$800

time the actual unit cost gets larger than the budgeted unit cost, a flag goes up that an apparent problem exists.

The job-control report formats illustrated in Figures 4-3, 4-4, and 4-5 have the ability to satisfy the first four elements of an effective control system. These control elements are

1. A *timely*
2. comparison of *actual*
3. versus *plan* (or budget)
4. to detect a *potential problem.*

When the percentage of effort for a work activity is greater than the percentage of work completed, there are at least six explanations or reasons. If the control system is to be effective, it is critical that the residential builder investigate the reasons for the overrun. Each of the reasons listed below should result in a follow-up action.

1. Productivity problem

There may be one of many productivity problems occurring; for example, inadequate supervision, understaffing of the work, poor worker attitudes, etc. If productivity is the reason, the project-control report identifies or flags this and the contractor should attempt to correct it immediately. Some problems like inadequate or improper supervision can be addressed. Other problems, like inclement weather, may be more difficult to address.

2. *Estimating problem*

There may be no onsite problem; the problem may be that the estimate of labor productivity was too optimistic. If this is the case, the residential builder should recognize this fact and incorporate the information into future estimates.

3. *Inadequate record keeping*

The fact that the report indicates more hours expended for the Form Slabs than should have occurred to date may be the result of intentional or unintentional inaccurate jobsite record keeping. For example, the foreman may have filled out daily timecards inaccurately by charging craft-hours to the wrong work code. If this is the case, the record-keeping process should be improved.

4. *Improper method of handling change orders*

The contractor is often required to do additional work via a change order process. For example, additional concrete work may have been assigned to the firm. In doing this work, the residential builder would update their actual labor hours and work quantities performed. However, they may not have updated the estimate and therefore the percentages illustrated for the labor hours expended and quantity of work placed are wrong. If this is the reason for the apparent error in matching the percentages, the change-order process should be corrected; the budget's and the actual's quantities and hours must be updated for change orders.

5. *Improper or poor list of work item codes*

The job-control report should be set up so that if the residential builder is 50 percent finished with a work item and everything is going as planned, then 50 percent of the labor hours should have been expended. It may be that the reason for the apparent problem with the Form Slab work item is that the firm has a bad list of work items. For example, the work codes could be defined too broadly. If this is the case, the firm should redefine the work codes in the cost system.

6. Changed work conditions or a claim

It may be that the residential builder is being required to do the concrete wall work under changed or unexpected work conditions (for example, the work is being impacted by an obstruction). The residential builder may be entitled to extra payment for the changed condition or may initiate a claim. If this is the case, this should be documented so that the claim can be negotiated. The job-control report can support this with documentation.

The job-control report is only effective if overruns are investigated and attempts are made to correct overruns. One way the residential builder can force the "reaction" to the job-control report would be to require the onsite supervisor to formally respond (with a short written report) as soon as the variance is projected.

Focusing on Under-budget Work Items and Variation

It also is important for the residential builder to investigate under runs as well as overruns. It is fairly common for a firm to place considerable emphasis on investigating problems, identifying the cause, and reprimanding the guilty individual. However, it also is important to spend time identifying reasons why various work items on the job-control report are under budget.

For example, for the roofing work item in Figure 4-3, the item is projected to come under budget by 40 man-hours. Just like there are reasons why a work item is over budget, there has to be a reason why the work item is under budget. By spending time with the supervisor who beats the budget for various work items, the cause can be identified and attempts made to duplicate the success. The residential builder should attempt to eliminate reasons for problems and duplicate successes. The job-control report can be useful in meeting both of the objectives.

An addition to the typical job-control report also can aid the residential builder by measuring the risk of the various work performed. Risk can be defined as variation from the average. A column can be added to the job-control report shown in Figure 4-3 that reports the productivity achieved this week relative to either that which was achieved last week or the average achieved to date. The reader of the report will soon be able to sense the productivity risk for individual work items. The productivity variation from one week to another will likely be much higher for work such as forming concrete than for work such as placing the rebar or concrete. It is important for the residential builders to be aware of productivity and/or cost risk so that they can assign the appropriate degree of supervision to the work task.

Extending the Job-control report to Monitor Project Time

The job-control report can be extended to monitor project time as well as cost. Budgeting and measuring actual crew size per work item or activity as well as quantity of work and labor hours can do this. Consider the data shown in Figure 4-3. By adding the budgeted crew sizes and the actual crew sizes as shown in Figure 4-6, the residential builder has a means of monitoring project time and cost.

The format of this job-control report enables forecasting of the variation of activity hours (or cost) and duration. For example, for the "Forming" activity shown in Figure 4-6, there is a forecasted overrun in hours or cost. Based on the work being 50 percent complete, it will take 700 hours to complete all the work-a 200-hour overrun relative to the 500-hour budget.

On the other hand, owing to the larger-than-planned crew for this Forming activity, there is a forecasted variance of –3.75 days (the

FIGURE 4-6 Job-control Report for Project Time and Cost

Name of Work Item	Bud-geted Quan-tity	Bud-geted Hours	Bud-geted Crew	Planned Dura-tion Days	Actual Quan-tity	Actual Hours	Actual Crew	Fore-casted Dura-tion	% Work Done	% Hours	Fore-cast Var. Hours	Fore-cast Vary Time Days
Form	500	500	5	12.5	250	350	10	8.75	50	70	+200	-3.75
Carpen-try	300	300	6	6.25	100	150	5	7.5	50	50	—	+1.25
Roofing	100	200	4	6.25	50	80	4	5	50	40	-40	-1.25

work is projected to take 3.75 days less than budgeted). The above analysis assumes an eight-hour workday. Given a crew size of 10 workers (instead of the budgeted five), the workers will expend 80 hours per day. Dividing this into the forecasted total 700 man-hours of work, a projected duration of 8.75 days results. The end result is that while a man-hour or cost overrun is projected, the analysis indicates the work will actually take less time than budgeted.

It is important for the residential builder to monitor project time and cost for each work item. Just because a specific work item is on or under budget in regard to labor hours or labor cost, does not necessarily mean it will be finished within the allotted time budgeted as indicated on the project schedule. If the work item is behind schedule, the overall project will be impacted, leading to an added cost (for example, the project may be delayed and the contractor will incur a liquidated damage cost). As a work item or activity is in progress, one of four situations is possible:

1. The activity can be on or under the cost budget, and be on or under the time budget.
2. The activity can be over the cost budget, and over the time budget.
3. The activity can be over the cost budget, and on or under the time budget.
4. The activity can be on or under the cost budget, and over the time budget.

In the latter three situations, either a time or cost problem exists. The residential builder should react to the problem and implement immediate procedures to reduce or eliminate the problem.

The above extension of the job-control report is only possible if the job cost "work items" are defined to be the same as the project schedule activities and vice versa. This integrating of the job-control system and the scheduling system is discussed in the following section.

Integrating Estimating, Scheduling, and the Control Function

To gain efficiency and accuracy in performing the estimating, scheduling, and control functions, an integrated approach should be taken; in other words, each of the functions should be performed in conjunction with one another by using a common set of work packages. A work item for estimating should be an activity on the project schedule and should be a cost object in the control system.

This integrated system can be illustrated with an example using the work package of "Erecting Concrete Foundation Wall Forms."

1. Historical database

We will assume that our example residential builder has performed previous projects on which he has collected data regarding the placement of slab forms. In particular, we will assume the historical data shown in Figure 4-7.

2. Determine the quantity of work for the new project

Let us assume our example residential builder is starting a new project, House 106. The estimator would systematically review the drawings and specifications and calculate the amount of work to be performed for the various defined work items. The calculations and calculated quantities of work are placed on an estimating form or sheet.

While a project would require that several different work items be performed for a project, we will focus on one. Let us assume that after doing the takeoff, the estimator has determined the following quantity of work:

Foundation Wall Forms = 20,000 square feet of contact area (sfca)

FIGURE 4-7 Historical Data for Placing Slab Forms

Project Performed	Quantity of Wall Forms	Crew Size Utilized	Person-hours Expended	Person-hours/ square foot	Cumulative Person-hours/sfca
House 101	10,000 sfca	20	1,000	0.10	0.10
House 102	12,000 sfca	12	1,050	0.0875	0.0932
House 103	20,000 sfca	15	1,600	0.08	0.0869
House 104	9,000 sfca	13	800	0.0888	0.869
House 105	20,500 sfca	25	2,700	0.132	0.100
	71,500 sfca		7,150		0.100

3. Review past data, select method, and determine man-hours required

As a basis of planning the method and determining the cost and duration, the residential builder should review past historical data, determine the crew size to be used, and determine the required man-hours that will be needed.

The review of past data indicates that the man-hours required per square foot of contact area of forms placed has varied between 0.08 person-hours per sfca and 0.132 person-hours per sfca. In order to help in determining estimated man-hours per sfca for the work to be done for House 106, the residential builder would decide on how many workers he or she is going to assign to the work. Let us assume that based on a study of the historical data and the work to be done, the residential builder decides on the following:

$$\text{Crew size} = 20 \text{ workers}$$
$$\text{Man-hours/sfca} = 0.10 \text{ person-hours/sfca}$$

Given the estimate of 0.10 person-hours/sfca, it follows that the total person-hours that will be required for House 106 is calculated as follows:

$$\text{Person-hours required} = (20,000 \text{ sfca}) \times (0.10 \text{ person-hours/sfca})$$
$$= 2,000 \text{ man-hours}$$

4. Determine planned or estimated cost

Assuming one knows the hourly wage rate for a worker, the labor cost can easily be determined by multiplying the required man-hours times the wage rate. Assume the wage rate is $21 per hour.

$$\text{Estimated Labor Cost} = (2,000 \text{ person-hours}) \times (\$21/\text{hr})$$
$$= \$42,000$$

5. Determining planned duration and project planning and scheduling

If the quantity of work, the estimated productivity, and the crew size are known (or estimated), the activity duration can be determined as follows:

$$\text{Duration} = (20{,}000 \text{ sfca}) \times \frac{(0.10 \text{ person-hours/sfca})}{(20 \text{ persons/person-hour})} = 100 \text{ hours}$$

$$\text{Duration} = \frac{(100 \text{ hours})}{(8 \text{ hours/day})} = 12.5 \text{ days (say 13 days)}$$

The duration for each and every activity would be determined in a similar way. The point is that the schedule durations are a byproduct of the estimating process; scheduling and estimating are done in conjunction with one another.

6. *Project control*

As the project progresses, productivity is measured against the project plan in an attempt to control the project. This can be done by comparing the actual person-hours per unit of work performed versus the planned or estimated person-hours per unit of work.

To illustrate this process, let us assume that after several days, jobsite records indicate the following:

Quantity of work in place = 5,000 sfca
Man-hours expended   = 1,000 person-hours

The supervisor can monitor the work and productivity by either comparing the percentage of work completed to the percentage of person-hours expended, or by comparing the person-hours per unit of work performed versus the budgeted man-hours per unit of work performed.

$$\text{Percentage of Work Put in Place} = \frac{\text{Quantity of Work Put in Place}}{\text{Budgeted Quantity}}$$

$$\text{Percentage of Work Put in Place} = \frac{5{,}000 \text{ sfca}}{20{,}000 \text{ sfca}} = 0.25 \text{ or } 25\%$$

$$\text{Percentage of Effort Expended} = \frac{\text{Expended Person-hours to Date}}{\text{Budgeted Person-hours}}$$

$$\text{Percentage of Effort Expended} = \frac{1{,}000 \text{ Person-hours}}{2{,}000 \text{ Person-hours}} = 0.50 \text{ or } 50\%$$

The fact that it has taken 50 percent of the man-hour budget to do 25 percent of the work will alert the residential builder to a productivity problem. Analysis of the problem will make it possible to correct the problem.

7. Update past project data

The control process described above would be ongoing. Many firms generate a control report weekly or monthly to monitor the productivity. When the project is completed, the past project productivity data would be updated to reflect the results of the most recent project.

Let us assume that House 106 is completed. Based on jobsite records, the final quantities and man-hours expended are as follows:

Quantity of Work Performed = 20,000 sfca
Person-hours Expended = 3,000 man-hours

The past project productivity data would be updated as shown in Figure 4-8:

Given another project to plan and estimate, the process described starts again. Past project data becomes the database for planning and estimating new projects. Estimating, planning and scheduling, and control become part of an integrated project management system.

FIGURE 4-8 Updated Historical Data for Placing Slab Forms

Project Performed	Quantity of Wall Forms	Crew Size Utilized	Person-hours Expended	Person-hours/ square foot	Cumulative Person-hours/sfca
House 101	10,000 sfca	20	1,000	0.10	0.10
House 102	12,000 sfca	12	1,050	0.0875	0.0932
House 103	20,000 sfca	15	1,600	0.08	0.0869
House 104	9,000 sfca	13	800	0.0888	0.869
House 105	20,500 sfca	25	2,700	0.132	0.100
House 106	20,000 sfca	20	3,000	0.150	0.1109
Totals	**91,500 sfca**		**10,150**		

Input or Performance Management

This chapter has emphasized the control of project time and cost by comparing actual performance against budgeted performance. In particular, as shown in Figure 4-3, the percentage of effort (expressed in craft labor hours) is compared to the percentage of work put in place. Such a system is much more effective than merely comparing labor hours against the budgeted labor hours. However, both systems can be viewed as being "results" oriented. Attention is drawn to a problem after the problem occurs.

An alternative to the typical job-control system is what the author refers to as input or performance management or control. In this system of control, the residential builder shifts from results to setting out and monitoring input. For each work item or work task, the contractor would set out the crew size required to do the work. The control focus would then monitor daily the actual crew size.

For example, for the work item "Form" illustrated in Figure 4-6, 500 craft-hours were budgeted. Assume the work was to be performed in 12.5 days, and that a worker is scheduled to work eight hours a day. The craft-hours required each day for the 12.5 days is calculated as follows:

$$\text{Craft- or person-hours required per day} = \frac{500 \text{ craft-hours}}{12.5 \text{ days}}$$
$$= 40 \text{ craft-hours per day}$$

The number of workers that would be needed every day is then calculated as follows:

$$\text{Number of workers needed per day} = \frac{40 \text{ craft-hours per day}}{8 \text{ hours per worker}} = 5$$

The five workers become the key control element in the input or performance management approach. The residential builder would proceed to monitor the presence of the five workers each day. The first day that five workers are not present, it follows that the work will not be done in the budgeted 12.5 days.

This control approach would appear especially appropriate for monitoring a subcontractor's performance. By getting the residential builder to set out how he is going to get something done, the firm can then hold him to it. Instead of coming down on the firm when it fails to meet a promised completion date, the residential builder would monitor the subcontractor's effort. The premise is simple: if the effort is not made, the results will not happen.

Record Keeping and Control

The job-control reports discussed in this chapter are only as good as the data on the source documents that provide information to the reports. These source documents include the daily timecards and daily or weekly reports that summarize the project quantities put in place.

Often the residential builder's projects are quite distant from the firm's main office. In addition, many jobsite personnel may favor the production function over the field-reporting function. Many firms have difficulty getting time and accurate jobsite data to support the control function. In fact, inaccurate or late jobsite data often are characteristic of the entire construction industry.

Inaccurate or late field reports do not have to be part of the construction process. In fact, it is critical that the residential builder obtain accurate and timely field data, including timecards and quantity reports. How can this be achieved?

Construction foremen and superintendents often are the individuals required to submit the data that serves as the basis of the job-control report. When requesting these individuals to fill out job forms, it is important for the residential builder to remember and implement the following three rules:

1. No one should fill out forms unless they know where the data goes, why it is needed, and how it is used.
2. No one should fill out forms unless they are shown, by example, that the data is in fact used.
3. No one should fill out forms unless they are given a feedback report (either written or oral) for every form they fill out.

The importance of accurate and timely record keeping should be emphasized with all workers. The residential builder should consider giving recognition or even an award to individuals that fill out accurate and timely reports. Awards often are given for worker years of service, safety, etc. Given the importance of the control function, an award for accurate and timely record keeping seems equally important.

The very design of field reports affects the accuracy of the data on the field reports. For example, if the firm uses a weekly timecard, the foreman will likely procrastinate and only fill it out on the fifth day, unsuccessfully trying to recall what workers did two or three days ago. A daily timecard will force daily recording of data. In addition, the person filling out the form should easily understand work codes on the timecard. Forms that require field personnel to simply check items rather than write long narratives are preferred, given the time pressures of the field personnel. The residential builder should always follow the premise that field personnel are production people, not accountants. Anything that can be done to make the field reporting easier should be done.

5

Eliminating Productivity Defects at the Project

The residential builder has historically used the accounting process to monitor project productivity and costs. The residential builder uses past project data to estimate future projects and then proceeds to monitor the budget by recording field labor hours and labor costs against the budget. This process is illustrated in Figure 5-1.

The project control function illustrated in Figure 5-1 is accomplished by breaking down a project into work items and monitoring the process via a job-control report such as that shown in Figure 5-2. For purposes of an example, only a few work items are shown. This process was discussed in detail in a prior chapter on project control.

The "actual quantities" come from the job-control diaries or job-site reports as the project progresses. Similarly, the "actual labor hours" comes from the daily or weekly project time cards. The "projected over or under hours" is determined by a linear comparison of the percentage of quantities in place to the labor hours expended to date. For example, if it took 450 labor hours to complete 50 percent of the work (250 of the 500 units are in place), it follows that it will take a total of 900 labor hours to complete all of the work—a 100 labor-hour overrun.

The residential builder monitors the job-control report shown as a management tool for project control. In addition, the data collected indirectly becomes part of a database for estimating future work. For example, for the project illustrated, the 1000 units of walls

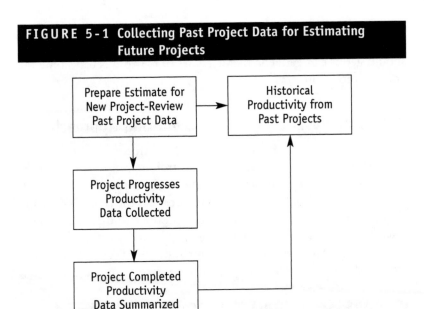

FIGURE 5-1 Collecting Past Project Data for Estimating Future Projects

were completed using 995 field labor hours. It follows that on the next project the estimator is likely to use a production rate of 0.995 field labor hours per unit of wall work when estimating the labor effort required for constructing walls. In effect, past project data becomes a source of information for estimating work.

While the above-described process is good for project control, by itself it will not promote improvement. In fact, the process actually promotes the benchmarking of inefficiencies. When using the

FIGURE 5-2 Example Job-control Report

Work Activity	Quantity	Units	Estimated Quantity	Estimated Hours	Actual Quantity	Actual Hours	Projected Overrun/ (Underrun) in Hours

accounting process described, the residential builder is in effect benchmarking what productivity they are getting, not what they should get or can get. The inefficiencies of past projects become the goals of future projects.

Defect Analysis Versus the Accounting Approach

There definitely is a need to implement an effective control system such as that shown in Figure 5-2 for controlling projects. Obviously, knowing the status of projects relative to the budget is important. However, it also is important to remember that the typical construction project includes considerable nonproductive time that can be traced to what the author refers to as "productivity defects."

Figure 5-3 shows an example breakdown of work states for a worker during an eight-hour day at a construction project. Obvi-

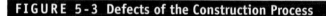

FIGURE 5-3 Defects of the Construction Process

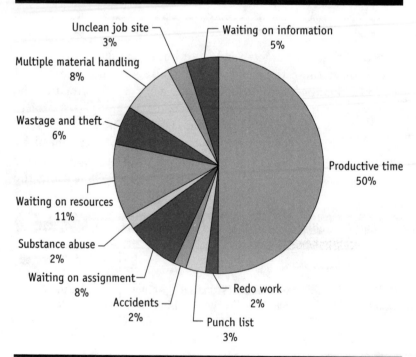

Unclean job site
3%

Waiting on information
5%

Multiple material handling
8%

Wastage and theft
6%

Productive time
50%

Waiting on resources
11%

Substance abuse
2%

Waiting on assignment
8%

Accidents
2%

Punch list
3%

Redo work
2%

ously, the percentage of time for each of the work states shown varies from project to project. However, the illustration is fairly typical of the construction process; it might be referred to as the "four-hour" construction workday. This is not to say that workers want to be nonproductive. Often, the fault can be traced to the onsite supervisor. For example, a large percentage of the nonproductive waiting time illustrated can often be traced to the supervisor's failure to plan and schedule. The benefits of planning and scheduling were discussed in a prior chapter.

It should be noted that the worker illustrated in Figure 5-3 is only in a productive state approximately 50 percent of the workday. Productive work can mean "doing work that is absolutely necessary to completing the project;" for example, putting in a concrete block, properly performing carpentry framing work, etc. The rest of the time the worker is in a nonproductive state doing redo work, doing punch list work, waiting on a supervisor to tell him or her what to do, handling material unnecessarily, waiting on resources, looking for a tool or material, etc. It is interesting to note that most workers normally do not like to be in many of the nonproductive work states any more than the residential builder likes to pay them for the time. Most workers dislike redo work, punchlist work, double handling of materials, waiting, etc.

The "defects" tend to become commonplace on construction projects. In effect they are budgeted or estimated. The end result is that when the residential builder observes that he or she beat the budget for a work item in Figure 5-2 by five hours relative to the 1,000 labor-hour budget, he or she should not feel good about it; in effect, he or she just came close to duplicating the four-hour work day.

A Proactive Program for Improvement of a Defect

Residential builders need a proactive program to improve jobsite productivity through the measurement of defects. Consistent with the practice of Total Quality Management (TQM), it is proposed that one cannot improve or eliminate a defect unless one measures the defect and investigates the causes of it. The process of continuous improvement is illustrated in Figure 5-4.

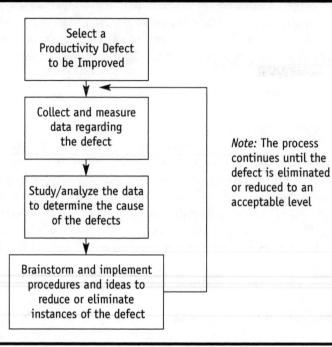

FIGURE 5-4 Continuous Improvement Cycle

Select a
Productivity Defect
to be Improved

Collect and measure
data regarding
the defect

Study/analyze the data
to determine the cause
of the defects

Brainstorm and implement
procedures and ideas to
reduce or eliminate
instances of the defect

Note: The process
continues until the
defect is eliminated
or reduced to an
acceptable level

Step 1. Select a Defect to Improve

It is unlikely that the firm will be able to initially or simultaneously measure or attack each of the defects shown in Figure 5-3. Instead, it is proposed that the residential builder initially focus on one defect. By focusing on the measurement, identification of causes, and elimination of the causes for a single defect for a time period (say a year or two), the firm can focus everyone's attention on the need to reduce or eliminate the defect.

When selecting the defect to measure, analyze, and reduce (if not eliminate), the residential builder should consider the following:

- Which defect is causing the most nonproductive time for typical firm projects?
- How easy is it to gather data regarding the number of incidences of the defect and the cause of the defect?

- How easy is it to improve the productivity defect (i.e. which defect can the firm expect to obtain improvement more quickly and be able to measure the improvement)?

Step 2. Collect and Measure Data Regarding the Defect

Once the defect is selected, the residential builder should develop a form or procedure for measuring incidences of the defect at the project site. In some cases this may mean simply adding a new cost code like redo work or material handling. In other cases it may mean creating a new procedure or form for developing a random testing/measurement program to check on incidences of the defect.

Data can be collected in many ways and creativity should be used to collect it. The data can be collected continually or by using a random data collection process.

Various data collection models include the following:

- Time study techniques
- Work sampling techniques
- Productivity rating models
- Crew balance models
- Method productivity delay model

These and other industrial engineering-type models are described in many textbooks. If used properly, they do not intimidate workers. Just because residential builders have not used them extensively in the past does not mean they cannot be used. It is important that the residential builder retain the right to manage. He or she should use data collection models with the philosophy that the data is being collected to identify improvement, not to blame people. If workers feel they are being measured in order to be blamed, human nature will have it that they will frown on the approach. However, if the approach is one of improvement-i.e. working smarter, not harder-the measurement process will be accepted.

Flowcharting work methods are another way of analyzing the work process and identifying incidences of the productivity defect. Using simple flowchart symbols such as those in

Figure 5-5 will enable the residential builder to identify improvement potential.

The residential builder might even consider the use of a second timecard for collecting data-a "defect timecard"—such as the form shown in Figure 5-6. Instead of only focusing on measuring labor hours against the budget or estimate, the builder may want to attempt to measure project defect time. By measuring defect time, identifying the causes, and addressing the causes, the firm will be able to reduce if not eliminate the defect.

Admittedly, the use of a timecard such as that shown in Figure 5-6 or the use of one or more of the data collection models noted above is not the "norm" at the residential builder's jobsite. However, just because it has not been the "norm" doesn't mean it cannot be useful. All one has to do is look at the high percentage of nonproductive time illustrated in Figure 5-3 and one can argue that new techniques, procedures, and ideas need to be tried.

Step 3. Studying the Cause for the Incidences of the Defect

As noted above, data regarding incidences of a defect are not collected merely to blame or to point a finger at individuals. The data are collected to focus on causes and to identify means of

FIGURE 5-5 Flowchart Symbols

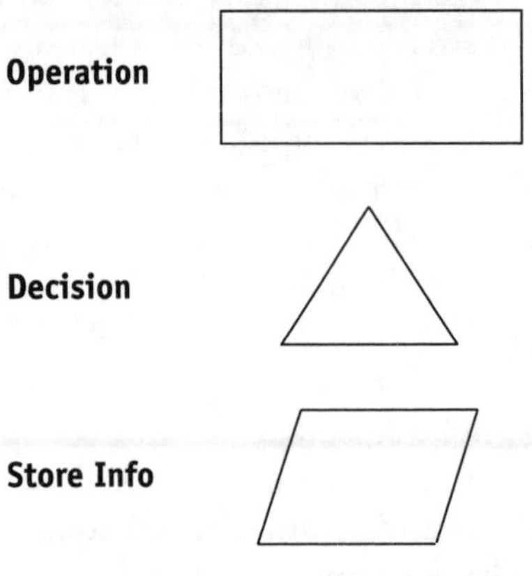

Operation

Decision

Store Info

FIGURE 5-6 Timecard for Recording Defect Time

Project _____ Supervisor _____ Date _____

Cost Code	Worker	Worker	Worker	Worker	Worker	Worker	Total Hours
Productive time							
Redo work							
Punch work							
Accidents							
Waiting on assignment							
Substance abuse							
Waiting on resources							
Wastage and theft							
Multiple material handling							
Unclean jobsite							
Waiting on information							
TOTALS FOR DAY							

improvement. When an incidence of a defect occurs, the cause of the defect must also be identified. For example, in the case of an incidence of redo work, the cause may be one of the following:

- Worker not given proper instructions
- Worker did not have proper skills
- Worker did not have proper tools
- Worker did not have proper materials

- Another work trade or the owner/designer caused the damage requiring redo work
- Work not properly inspected

The supervisor can obtain the above type of data by taking random observations or by using newly designed forms that report on the defect. No matter how the data are collected, it should be emphasized to the workers that it is for purposes of improvement, not to blame individuals for nonproductive time.

The collected data regarding a defect should be charted and analyzed. A histogram such as shown in Figure 5-7 might be used to chart the collected data.

Step 4. Brainstorming for Improvement

Having collected the information regarding the incidences of the defect and the causes, the residential builder can hold brainstorming meetings to address improvement ideas. Brainstorming can entail getting several different individuals together and hav-

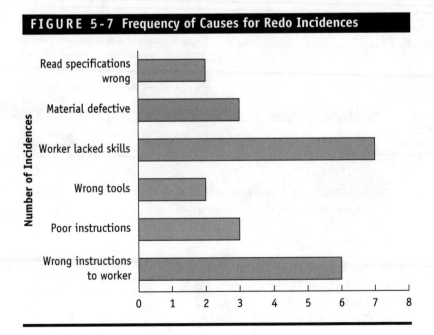

FIGURE 5-7 Frequency of Causes for Redo Incidences

ing them study the collected data in order to stimulate creative thinking of improvement options. Individuals should be encouraged to consider new ideas and to think outside of the box. For example, perhaps a sign like the one in Figure 5-8 can be posted at the jobsite to bring attention to the firm's objective of reducing the defect. Just because such a sign is not common at jobsites does not mean it cannot contribute to productivity. Sometimes the best idea is the strangest idea.

Once new ideas and procedures are decided upon, they should be implemented to determine if they work. Not all new ideas or procedures will yield results, but the residential builder cannot tell unless new ideas are tried. Once the new idea or procedure is implemented, the measurement process should continue and the cycle repeats itself as illustrated in Figure 5-4. The process or cycle continues, thus the term "continuous improvement."

It should be emphasized that the increased focus on measurement is not to place blame on individuals. Instead, the focus should be on team problem solving. The emphasis should be

FIGURE 5-8 Sign at Jobsite Measuring Incidences of Redo Work

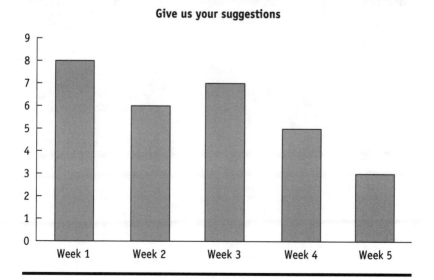

Give us your suggestions

on proactive management to reduce defects rather than the reaction to problems, similar to a fire drill.

As the residential builder achieves a commitment to reduce a selected defect and reduces the defect to zero or an acceptable number, the firm can select another defect to focus on. The point is that the defects will become standards unless they are measured, analyzed, and corrected. The concept of zero defects is not theory. The residential builder has likely constructed a project with zero defects; for example, zero hours of redo work or zero hours of doubling handling of material. Given that they have done it is evidence that it should be the goal on all the projects!

Implementing "MORE" Productivity

The traditional role of the construction supervisor is often viewed as one of monitoring or policing the residential project and the various work tasks that make up the project. As part of this monitoring role, the supervisor performs the following:

- Monitors onsite workers to make sure they are doing work
- Monitors material flow to make sure material is delivered to the proper locations when needed
- Monitors the project schedule to compare actual progress against planned progress
- Monitors and reviews job-control reports to update unit costs and productivity as the work progresses
- Monitors equipment use to make sure that the equipment is used efficiently and is in proper working order
- Monitors quality of work performed
- Monitors the work process to ensure that the work is performed safely

Another way of viewing the supervisor's traditional role as a monitor or policeman is to view the traditional job-cost preparation and review process shown in Figure 6-1.

When using the job-cost control process illustrated in Figure 6-1, the supervisor monitors labor hours against the budgeted labor hours relative to percentage of work put in place at the time. For example, if

FIGURE 6-1 Traditional Monitoring Role of the
                Construction Supervisor

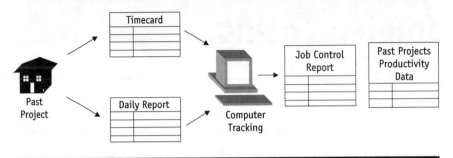

the report indicates that 25 percent of the labor hours have been expended but only 20 percent of work is in place, the supervisor's attention is drawn to this problem and he or she pursues a proper correction. After completion of the project, the results are summarized and become part of the database that is used by the estimator for future bids on new projects.

The traditional monitoring role of the supervisor shown in Figure 6-1 can also be viewed as the "accounting cycle" approach to productivity. Time cards, quantity reports, and the job-control report are the core of the approach. Such an approach focuses on preserving or maintaining the labor productivity budget. Past performances become the target for future projects.

The traditional or accounting approach is critical to being a good supervisor. The supervisor needs to be well versed in the process and should be schooled in providing proper input to the process and should be able to interpret and use various reports produced by the process.

While the traditional or accounting approach is an excellent process for the purpose of control, this approach does little to stimulate increased productivity. The traditional or accounting approach to supervision would be all that is necessary if the typical project was near or at optimal productivity. Every residential unit and every construction work task typically has significant potential for productivity improvement.

To significantly increase construction productivity, the supervisor needs to take a new and more proactive approach to supervision. One of these approaches is referred to as "MORE," an acronym for the author's approach to productivity improvement. The letters MORE represent the following four skills or approaches to supervising construction:

Measurement or benchmarking
Opportunity for improvement through challenging the work process
Risk analysis for productivity improvement
Estimating costs to improve focus on improvement

The MORE approach attempts to put the supervisor in a more proactive role by challenging the work process. Unlike the traditional approach to supervision that uses timecards, quantity reports, and job-control reports, the MORE approach can be viewed as using the tools shown in Figure 6-2.

MORE does not entail "time and motion" studies of workers. Admittedly, such an approach might intimidate the supervisor's workers. However, the supervisor does have a right to critique, to analyze, and to look for better ways to do things. The following sections address the four skills of MORE individually.

Measurement or Benchmarking

The premise of the measurement component of MORE is that measurement is fundamental to improvement. The measurement component will draw the supervisor's attention to inefficiencies and improvement potential.

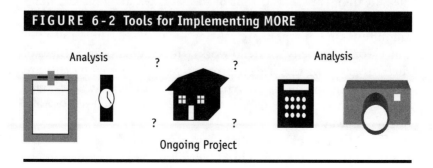

FIGURE 6-2 Tools for Implementing MORE

Analysis   ?   ?   Analysis

?   ?

Ongoing Project

- How many labor hours were expended on the residential project for punchlist work?
- How many hours was a laborer in a nonproductive work state versus that of a mason on the same project?
- How many instances were there of double handling of materials on a specific project?
- Do we get more square feet of contact area of wall forming done in the morning or afternoon?
- Do we get higher productivity for placing sheet metal ductwork on Tuesday or on Wednesday?
- How many picks do we get per hour with a crane?

The above are examples of questions that the supervisor cannot normally answer because he or she typically does not pay attention to measuring things. Instead he or she monitors or polices the work process. As long as the productivity is similar to that proposed in the budget, the supervisor likely feels satisfied. If the above issues were measured, the supervisor would likely find variation and causes that could lead to improvement.

Measurement is not proposed as a means of "placing blame" or simply to gather data. Measurement is a means of focusing on causes of variation and low productivity. For example, there has to be a reason why two similar projects have a different amount of redo hours expended per labor hour of effort on the project. Something must have been done right on one project that was not done on the other project. By measuring the incidences of redo work on the two projects, the reason for the variation can be studied and addressed for overall improvement.

In the MORE approach, the construction supervisor is asked to measure things or events that he or she has taken for granted. Things or events can be as simple as the distance material is moved, the amount of time foremen are waiting on material, the number of times work is done twice (redo work), the number of incidences of theft, or anything that affects productivity. The measurement can be done by timing things or events with a wristwatch, by taking random visual samples, or via new reporting that measures non-productive time by cause.

The key is to force the supervisor to become proactive through the measurement process. This attention to measurement will not require significant added personnel or added time for the supervisor. Instead of merely monitoring or watching, the supervisor can pick something to measure and make it part of his or her normal routine.

Consider a few examples:

Example 1. Studying a tower crane operation

A construction supervisor has concluded that much of the reason his project schedule has slipped relates to the use of a piece of equipment that moves materials vertically. The project progress is tied to the productive use of the machine, so the supervisor measured the number of "picks" of material the equipment was making per hour over a two-day period. The data is shown in Figure 6-3.

The average number of productive picks per hour was averaging a little over eight for the two days. However, by observing

FIGURE 6-3 Number of Machine "Picks" Over a Two-Day Period

No. of picks per hour	Day 1 (Comments)	No. of picks per hour	Day 2 (Comments)
5	Waiting on person to hook pick	4	Difficult to reach material
12		10	
6	Moved water bucket and scrap material	14	
15		4	Waiting on person to hook pick
4	Operator took short break	6	Waiting on person to hook pick
12		5	Operator took short break
6	Waiting on person to hook pick	9	
6		12	
Avg. =	8.25	Avg. =	8

and measuring the pick cycles, it was obvious that the total production output was being significantly curtailed by not having a worker at the machine where the material had to be hooked. Instead, the equipment operator (and the crew waiting on material) frequently waited while an individual walked to the location where the machine needed to be hooked.

It also became obvious as to the impact of the operator taking a break at an inopportune time or of the crane being used for tasks not assigned to it, such as moving the water bucket.

The supervisor figured out his crew cost per hour and concluded that every time the equipment made one fewer pick per hour it saved the project $240 in crew time and productivity. It became obvious to the supervisor that he was justified in hiring a worker at $30 per hour just to manage and hook the equipment movements. The supervisor also implemented a policy that the equipment was not to be used for unassigned work, such as moving the water bucket, when work was in progress.

One might think that the following suggestions should have been obvious to the supervisor without having to "measure" pick placements. The opposite may be true: Without stopping to measure and look, inefficiencies are more likely to become standards.

Example 2. Minimizing material handling

A sheet metal construction supervisor observed that her project was losing a considerable amount of time and money moving material from one location to another. While some of the material movement was the fault of other contractors getting in her way, she felt this was not the only reason. Therefore, she undertook a random process of tagging delivered material and asked anyone that moved the material to initial the tag and describe where the material was being moved. She explained to everyone that she was not doing this to blame anyone; she simply wanted to find out what was going on so that she and the workers could assess it.

After utilizing the measuring system for a month, she concluded that the average piece of ductwork material for the project was moved an average of 3.2 times before it was installed. This was excessive!

More importantly, the movement of the material could not always be placed with another trade. By measuring the material movement and the causes for the movement, she concluded the following:

- 24% of the extra movements related to another trade being in the way
- 26% of the extra movements related to the fact that their own support staff delivered or stored the material at the wrong location
- 18% of the extra movements related to the fact that the material was delivered too early and had to be moved because it got in the way
- 12% of the extra movements related to the fact that the wrong material was delivered to the site
- 8% of the extra movements related to the fact the material was not properly protected from adverse weather
- 12% of the extra movements could only be traced to normal construction operations

She noted that less than one-fourth of the extra or nonproductive material movements could be blamed on another trade. She also concluded that 64 percent of the extra nonproductive movements were in great part controllable by her own workers and her firm's actions or non-actions. She immediately took steps to reduce these causes resulting in a significant increase in productivity and a decrease in project duration. For example, more attention was given to proper material lay down areas, and subcontractors were held accountable for having materials in the way of other contractors.

In both of the examples, the supervisor's decision to measure rather than merely monitor was the difference between productivity improvement and letting inefficiencies become standards. The job-control report by itself did not disclose this potential productivity.

Opportunity for Improvement Through Challenging the Work Process

The second component of MORE is challenging the work process for the opportunity to improve. Almost always, there is more than one way to accomplish a work task. Different crew sizes, the use of different types of equipment, the use of alternative work methods, the substitution of different materials, and even the alternative times when a work task can be performed enable the construction supervisor to choose between several ways of accomplishing a work task. Each of the alternative ways of doing the work function will result in a different time and cost. In addition, depending on how a work task is performed, following work tasks may be affected positively or negatively. The process of challenging a work process looking for an opportunity to improve is a three-step process:

1. Familiarize oneself with the existing methods.
2. Conceptualize an alternative method. Sketch the proposed method on paper to better describe the proposed method.
3. Make total-cost, unit-cost, and duration calculations to compare the alternative methods.

The requirement to make the above analysis on an ongoing basis forces the supervisor to become conscious of looking for better ways to do things. His or her ability to determine a better work method is not guaranteed; however, the mere fact that the supervisor will take the time to consider alternatives will likely result in finding opportunity for improvement.

The supervisor can use several modeling techniques, such as time study and work sampling, to analyze and challenge a work process. However, the supervisor also can effectively challenge a work process by merely observing it and asking himself or herself a few questions. The supervisor should look at the current work process and ask the following questions:

- What is the work method?
- What are we trying to achieve?
- How are we currently doing the task?
- Why are we doing it this way?

- Who is best able to do the work?
- Where is the best place to do the work?
- When is the best time to do the task?

Asking these questions as one views a work process can lead to ideas for improving the work method. It helps to make notes and write down answers to each of these questions. It often requires several observations of several factors to understand or discover an opportunity for improvement. Observe the process, write down your observations, and then analyze the results.

Example 1. A framing operation

A supervisor is in charge of a carpentry framing operation. Because of the design of the structure, the framing members must be cut to a variety of specific lengths. In the current method, the lumber is stored by the side of the building and carried by a laborer (L) to a cutting location where a carpenter (C) cuts the studs to length on a cutting table. From the cutting location, two laborers carry the studs to carpenters (F) who nail the framing members into place. The current work process is shown in Figure 6-4.

Let us assume that the supervisor has noticed a significant amount of nonproductive time in the current work process. His first action is to observe the work process, ask himself the seven questions noted above, then write down his observations and answers.

- *What is the work method?*
  Stored lumber is carried to an onsite fabricating location, cut to length, then carried to two framing locations.
- *That are we trying to achieve?*
  The objective is to erect the framed structure quickly with a minimum of waiting time and material waste.
- *How are we currently doing the work task?*
  By cutting the studs at an onsite fabrication location, then carrying them to carpenters.
- *Why are we doing it this way?*
  Studs must be cut to a variety of specific lengths.

FIGURE 6-4 Existing Method for a Work Task

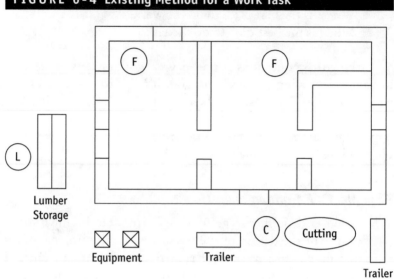

- *Who is best able to do this task?*
  This is a carpenter task—laborers carry the studs to the cutting site and to the carpenters.
- Where is the best place to do the task?
  Quality and cost effectiveness would improve if the studs were cut in the carpentry shop at the home office, or if they were precut before delivery from the supplier.
- When is the best time to do the task?
  There should be a supply of cut studs at the framing location before framing starts and throughout the framing operation.

By means of observing the work process, answering the questions, and analyzing the observations, the supervisor in our example discovered the following production delays or inefficiencies:

- Carpenters waiting on studs from laborers
- Laborers waiting on carpenters cutting studs
- Carpenters cutting studs waiting to receive material from storage

- Studs cut to wrong length; carpenter gives to laborer to take back to cutting location
- Considerable material wastage because of incorrect lengths
- Excessive walking to and from storage area and around equipment

The supervisor then developed and implemented several changes to the current method:

- Cut the lumber at the company's home office carpentry shop
- Color code the cut members by length
- Deliver cut lumber to the site
- At the site, store the cut studs at two locations that are near the framing operations
- Reduce the crew from two laborers to one laborer

The changed work method is illustrated in Figure 6-5.

The changes resulted in the five significant productivity benefits:

- Framing carpenters no longer wait for studs because an inventory of pre-cut, color-coded studs is nearby and available for delivery by a laborer (previously delay #1).
- There is no waiting at the onsite fabrication location because it has been eliminated (previously delays #2 and #3).
- Fewer pieces are returned to storage because they are rejected for incorrect length at the framing location (previously delay #4). This reduced time for workers waiting at the site.
- Material waste is reduced because quality control at the home office carpentry shop is better than at the on-fabrication location (previously delay #5).
- Number of laborers and walking time is reduced because the inventory of cut studs is closer to the framing locations and there are fewer rejected material pieces to be returned to storage.

Significant productivity improvement resulted in the changed method illustrated in Figure 6-5. This improvement resulted from simply challenging the work method.

FIGURE 6-5 Improved Method Determined Via Challenging the Work Process

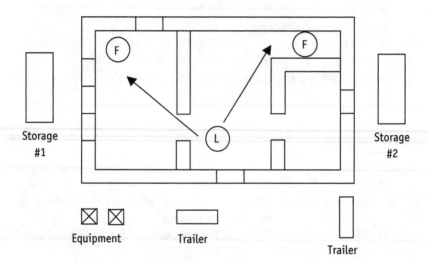

Changes
- ❏ Cut the lumber at the company's home office carpentry shop.
- ❏ Color code the cut studs by length.
- ❏ Deliver to the site.
- ❏ Store the cut studs at two locations nearby to the framing operation.
- ❏ Reduce the crew from two laborers to one laborer.

Results
- ❏ Framing carpenters no longer wait for studs.
- ❏ There is no waiting at the on-site fabrication location.
- ❏ Fewer pieces are returned to storage.
- ❏ Material waste is reduced.
- ❏ Number of laborers and walking time is reduced.

The carpenters and laborers in the original method (Figure 6-4) did not choose to be nonproductive. They may well have been hustling from one location to the next. The improved method results in the workers working smarter, not harder.

It should be noted that before the supervisor makes the changes shown, he or she also should evaluate the cost of the new method. For example, the cost for transporting the studs from the carpentry shop, the reduction in the crew size and waiting time, and the reduction in material waste are among factors to be considered.

The supervisor should challenge himself or herself weekly, if not daily, to look for opportunities to improve the work process. If the supervisor gets into the habit of challenging the work process and looking for opportunities, he or she will become a proactive supervisor rather than merely being reactive!

Monitoring or policing a work method can be viewed as a means of maintaining productivity. It is the challenging of the work process for opportunity that enables increased productivity!

Risk Analysis for Productivity Improvement

The construction process is subject to considerable uncertainty and risk. The productivity, cost, and duration of a work process is dependent on variable and unpredictable weather, variations in worker skills and attitudes, unexpected equipment breakdowns, changes in the difficulty or scope of work, etc.

Risk can be thought of as possible variation from expected or average results.

Example 1

Consider the two construction methods illustrated in Figure 6-6. Assume a supervisor has collected past project productivity data regarding two alternative ways of placing concrete (for example, using a concrete pump versus placing the concrete with a crane bucket). The points shown under the bell shaped curves represent the amount of concrete placed per worker-hour on past projects. While the past project data implies that both methods of placing the concrete have the same expected average produc-

FIGURE 6-6 Past Project Production Rate Samples

Comparison of Productivity Risk

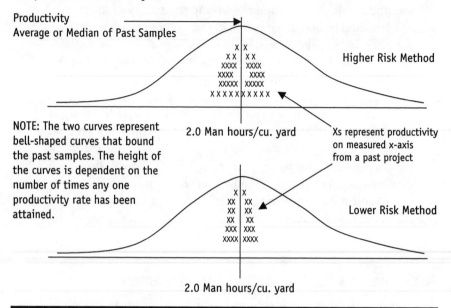

Productivity
Average or Median of Past Samples

Higher Risk Method

NOTE: The two curves represent bell-shaped curves that bound the past samples. The height of the curves is dependent on the number of times any one productivity rate has been attained.

2.0 Man hours/cu. yard

Xs represent productivity on measured x-axis from a past project

Lower Risk Method

2.0 Man hours/cu. yard

tivity, the past project data implies that the past data samples for Method 1 have varied more from the average than those for Method 2. Method 1 has more productivity risk.

One point to observe about measured risk is that the construction supervisor should pay extra attention to risk, as well as production and cost of production when managing construction. As an example of the misdirected effort of a supervisor, consider the following steps necessary to construct a concrete foundation wall:

1. Form the wall
2. Place reinforcing steel
3. Place concrete

Most everyone would agree that the work task shown above that has the most variation in units placed per time period or worker-hour (productivity) is the forming of the walls. Owing to the difficulty of such tasks of placing the forming ties, releasing the forms from the wall in the stripping operation, and bracing the forms, the square feet of contact area of forms placed varies significantly from one time period to the next.

While most construction supervisors would agree that the forming operation has the most variation in the work process and is therefore the riskiest work task, the fact remains that the placement of the concrete itself gets most of the construction supervisor's attention. The day that the concrete is being placed will be the day that everyone at the jobsite is watching the concrete fall from the concrete chute into the wall. On the other hand, the forming operation often goes unsupervised! An analysis of the job-control reports for the project would illustrate that the risk in the project schedule and the risk of the project cost is much greater with the forming work task than with the concrete placement work task.

The supervisor should focus on the productivity risk as well as production itself. Productivity data can be gathered and printed in the job-control reports that tracks productivity variation as well as average productivity. As a guide for the supervisor, the work tasks in the estimate might be categorized and prioritized by productivity risk. The intent is to draw the supervisor's attention to work tasks that must be closely planned and supervised. As part of his or her daily planning, the supervisor should use a worksheet to prioritize the risk of work tasks to be done during the day.

On a positive note, productivity variation or risk can be viewed as setting out the potential to improve.

Example 2

Let us assume the residential builder has kept data regarding the average number of craft-hours required to place 100 square feet of contact area (sfca) of forms for two different forming methods. The data are illustrated in Figure 6-7.

The variation in productivity from job to job is larger for Method 1 than it is for Method 2. The fact that variation in productivity for Method 1 is greater than for Method 2 may indicate the following:

FIGURE 6-7 Variation in Production Rate for Two Methods

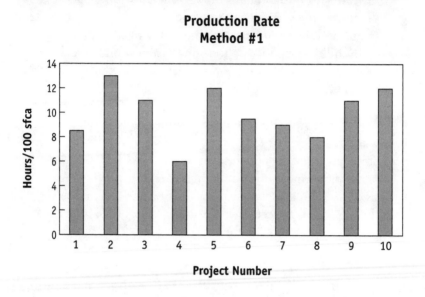

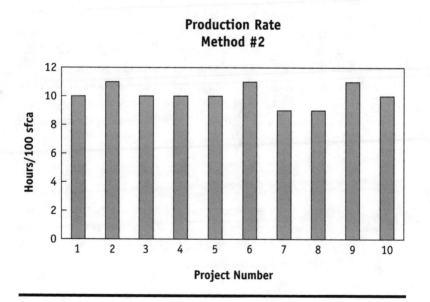

1. Method 1 is riskier than Method 2 in terms of productivity as a function of time. As such, Method 1 likely needs more supervising.
2. Method 1 may result in more variation in quality of the finished work. One can usually assume that if productivity is more variable, that the resulting quality of the finished construction is also more variable. For example, the quality of the wall finish may be more variable.
3. From a productivity improvement point of view, the fact that Method 1 has more productivity variation or risk leads one to the conclusion that this method has more potential for improvement. Inspection of the past productivity results for the two methods indicates that a production rate of 6 craft-hours per 100 sfca was attained when using Method 1. This was better than any production rate attained when using Method 2. By studying how this production rate was achieved, and by implementing the improved method, it may be that Method 1 can be improved to the point that the average production rates come within the range of 6 to 9 craft-hours per 100 sfca, better than the current average of 10.

By studying variation or risk, and by focusing on the production cycles that were better than average, it may be possible for the supervisor to improve the productivity rate for the method in question. Improvement may entail a reduction in the average craft-hours required and/or a reduction in productivity risk or variation.

Many examples can be given of how the study of productivity variation or risk can lead to the improvement of a work process. For example, the data shown in Figure 6-6 could also represent the following:

- Productivity attained in the morning versus afternoon
- Number of items on the punchlists for two different types of projects
- Number of incidences of workers waiting on material at two different projects

In summary, the supervisor should focus on the risk of work processes so that he or she can appropriate his or her time to supervising tasks correctly; the more risk in the work process, the more time the supervisor should expend supervising the task. Secondly, the supervisor should view risk as an opportunity to improve. By studying work conditions when productivity was good and studying the work conditions when productivity was bad, the supervisor can improve productivity. This can be done by duplicating the good conditions and reducing or eliminating the bad conditions.

Estimating Costs to Improve Focus on Improvement

The observer of the construction process may view the process as using different types of trained workers to place materials such as block and brick. However, another view is that everything that is being done in the construction of a project is a process of handling and placing money. Labor, materials, and equipment can be viewed in terms of dollars. In fact, one might propose that the supervisor is not managing concrete or steel placement-he or she is really managing money.

The supervisor's knowledge of the cost of things and resources such as labor is critical to his or her ability to properly manage. Consider two construction work tasks that may be scheduled for the same work day: one that has a unit cost of $5 per unit placed and one that has a unit cost of $50 per unit placed. Risk aside, if the supervisor can only be in one of two places, he or she had better be at the more expensive cost operation.

The above example of the supervisor choosing to be at the more expensive of the two operations appears obvious. However, sometimes it is not so obvious. The supervisor must know the cost of things if he or she is going to allocate his or her supervisor time.

Example 1

Consider a construction work method being observed. The observer might see two or three workers having a cigarette and become very upset with the nonproductive time of the workers. Assume the following worker wage rate:

Wage rate without fringe benefits for example
   worker   = $28.00/hr.
Wage rate with fringe benefits for example worker = $38.00/hr.

Given the fact that the observer views the three workers as costing anywhere from $28 to $38 dollars an hour, when the observer sees the workers taking a fifteen minute cigarette break, the observer sees the following nonproductive time or cost.

Nonproductive cost
per day owing to   = (3 workers) × (15 minutes or 1/4 hour)
unnecessary break   × ($38/hr)
                     = $285.00

This is a considerable sum of money. However, right next to the three nonproductive workers may be a crane or another type of equipment that hasn't moved or been productive in a two-hour time period. The crane likely rents for about $150/hour. Why doesn't the idle equipment get the same attention as the idle workers?

The answer is simple. Most observers of the construction process, including some supervisors, look at the equipment as metal, not money. The idle equipment, while wasting $300 in the above example, gets off easy at the expense of labor.

Consider this second example as to why it is important to know costs of things as well as to know what the thing is.

Example 2

An owner of the residential firm comes to a project and notices that there are concrete wedge bolts laying all over a jobsite. The concrete wedge bolts, which cost about $1 each, are used to connect concrete modular forms.

To get the supervisor's attention, the residential builder purchased 20 50-cent pieces. After lunch, the residential builder asked the supervisor to walk around the jobsite with him and, as they walked, he dropped the 50-cent pieces at various locations on the site.

At the end of the day, the contractor again asked the supervisor to walk the job again. Together they found only one of the 50-cent pieces (apparently overlooked by the workers). However, each and every wedge bolt was exactly were it was in the morning!

The above example merely points out that until people (including the supervisor) view things as money, they often are not attentive to them or mismanage them.

All too often there is a gap between the passing of cost information from the office to the supervisor. The supervisor may not have reviewed the estimate to determine what things cost and what are the high-cost-risk tasks for the project. In the MORE approach to supervising productivity, the supervisor's attention is focused on the cost of things and the cost of work tasks. For one, the cost estimate should be shared with the supervisor (this was discussed in the previous section of the course).

Secondly, the supervisor is well advised to carry an estimating cost book with him or her that sets out what things cost. Example cost data from one of the cost books is as shown in Figure 6-8.

The vocabulary of the construction industry tends to include terms like carpenter, concrete, crane, beam, or a forming panel. However, effective supervisors should expand their vocabulary to know what things cost, not just what they are. Given the requirement to be at more work task places than he or she can be every minute of the workday, all other things being equal, the supervisor should be where the money is!

FIGURE 6-8 Sample Cost Data

Item	$	Work Method	$
Carpenter	$30.00/per hour	Bulk excavation (labor, equipment)	$6.00/cubic yard
Concrete	$70/cubic	Place concrete (labor, material, equipment)	$180/cubic yard
Crane	$160/hour	Place electrical conduit (labor, material, equipment)	$12/linear foot
Steel beam	$1,500/ton	Place concrete block (labor, material, equipment)	$8/sq. foot
Modular forming panel	$180/panel	Place structural steel beam (labor, material, equipment	$4/dfca

7

Managing Equipment for Productivity Improvement

Productivity was defined in an earlier chapter as the following:

$$\text{Productivity} = \frac{\text{Units or Dollars of Output}}{\text{Person-hours of Input or Effort}}$$

However, productivity can be increased by means other than a person or persons working harder. Giving a worker a more productive piece of equipment or even replacing the worker with a machine or piece of equipment may increase productivity. Perhaps an improved definition of productivity would be the efficiency by which materials are placed using labor and equipment.

Admittedly, the residential builder is extremely dependent on the use of equipment. Many of the residential builder's projects can be constructed without the large pieces of equipment that road builders and commercial contractors may have at a jobsite. However, by focusing only on labor and ignoring equipment, the residential builder or supervisor does not get a true measure of total productivity or means to increase productivity. So why do supervisors typically pay more attention to labor productivity than they do to equipment productivity? One of the primary reasons likely relates to the fact that equipment is typically viewed as metal or machines, whereas labor is viewed as money.

Most laypersons know the approximate hourly wage rate of a construction worker. For example, even without all of the appropriate fringe benefits, the labor rate for a project craftsperson might be $25 per hour. Therefore, if the craftsperson is in a nonproductive state, such as waiting on materials for 15 minutes, it is easy to calculate that more than $6 has been wasted by nonproductive labor time.

The fact remains that often next to this idle craftsperson who is criticized for fifteen minutes of idle time is a machine that didn't move or do a productive activity for more than an hour. In many cases, the hourly rate (rental or ownership) for the equipment is greater than the hourly rate for the worker. For example, a crane may rent for more than $100 per hour. Nonetheless, idle equipment may not be the center of attention when the supervisor is looking for a means of increasing productivity. The reason is that the equipment is viewed as a machine or metal, when in fact it should be viewed as money.

One might suggest that if the hourly cost of owning or renting a piece of equipment was painted onto the machine, the supervisor would be more attentive to idle equipment time or nonproductive equipment activities. It is important for the supervisor to view equipment as money, not just as metal. Idle equipment is typically more costly than an idle craftsperson. The supervisor should make an effort to learn the hourly cost of equipment at his or her project in order to be more attentive to the cost of idle or nonproductive equipment.

Equipment Operating Costs Versus Ownership Costs

When a construction craftsperson works at a project for eight hours, he or she gets paid for eight hours. If the craftsperson is not at the project, he or she does not get paid. In other words, hourly labor costs can be viewed as a variable cost-they are paid as a function of activity.

On the other hand, equipment should be viewed as having two hourly cost components: an ownership cost and an operating cost. Even if equipment is not at a project (for example, the equipment might be idle at the company office), there is an hourly cost associated with it.

The hourly cost of owning and operating a piece of construction equipment is as shown below:

$$\begin{aligned} \text{Hourly cost} = \; &\text{Depreciation} + \text{Maintenance} + \text{Operating} \\ &+ \text{Repair} + \text{Finance} + \text{Insurance} + \text{Tax} \\ &+ \text{Replacement} \end{aligned}$$

A cost that increases as time increases is referred to as a cost that is a function of time-a **fixed** cost. When discussing construction equipment, this type of cost is referred to as an **ownership** cost. On the other hand, a cost that increases as the equipment is used to perform work is referred to as a **variable** cost. When discussing construction equipment, this type of cost is referred to as an **operating** cost.

The hourly cost components shown in the equation above will now be explained using the following example piece of construction equipment.

Example piece of equipment

Initial cost of equipment = $240,000
Estimated life of equipment in productive hours = 10,000 hours
Estimated salvage value of equipment at end of
useful life = $0
Interest or finance rate for borrowing money = 8%

A short explanation of each of the hourly cost components follows:

Depreciation

The ownership cost of purchasing a piece of equipment has to be charged to customers and projects through an hourly cost. Depreciation is the means by which the initial purchase cost is recovered. If the construction firm rents the equipment, the hourly rental rate includes the depreciation cost component.

There is some debate as to whether construction equipment wears out as a function of time or use; actually, to some degree, equipment wears out as a function of both time and use. However, more often than not, the value of construction equipment that moves materials is more dependent on how many hours the equipment has on the meter than on the age of the equipment. To the extent that a piece of equipment wears out as a function of time, it is an ownership cost; to the extent it wears out as a function of use, it is an operating cost.

For purposes of our example, let us assume that our $240,000 piece of equipment is judged to wear out as a function of use only. Given an estimated life of 10,000 productive hours of use, the hourly depreciation cost is calculated as follows:

$$\text{Depreciation cost (operating cost)} = \frac{\$240,000}{10,000 \text{ hours}} = \$24.00/\text{hour}.$$

Maintenance and operating costs

Maintenance and operating costs are similar in that they both occur as a function of equipment use. The more a piece of equipment is used, the more the maintenance and operating costs are incurred. Operating costs include expenses such as fuel and oil. Maintenance costs include lubrication, hoses, and tires. If the residential builder rents a piece of equipment, the rental agreement often requires the firm to pay for operating costs.

The best way to determine the maintenance and operating hourly costs for a piece of equipment is for the residential builder to keep records for these types of expenditures as a function of equipment use. Let us assume that for our example piece of equipment, the firm determines that the annual maintenance and operating costs are $7,000 and $9,000 respectively. Based on past records, the firm estimates 1,000 hours of productive use in a given year. The hourly maintenance and operating costs are therefore determined as follows:

$$\text{Maintenance cost (operating cost)} = \frac{\$7,000}{1,000 \text{ hours}} = \$7.00/\text{hour}$$

$$\text{Operating cost (operating cost)} = \frac{\$9,000}{1,000 \text{ hours}} = \$9.00/\text{hour}$$

It should be noted that lacking their own past records, the residential builder and supervisor can obtain approximate hourly maintenance and operating costs from the manufacturer of the equipment.

Repair costs

Repair costs differ from maintenance and operating costs in that repair costs are not ongoing—they are somewhat unpredictable and may occur sporadically. For example, it may be that the firm own-ing the $240,000 example piece of equipment has no repair costs for two years, only to have to repair the machine's undercarriage in year three at a cost of $30,000.

The hourly rate of a piece of equipment must include a reserve component set aside for paying repair costs. Even though the firm may not incur any repair costs during the first 2,000 hours of using a machine, the hourly rate charged to a customer during these first 2,000 hours has to include an hourly cost to establish a reserve for the repair costs.

As with maintenance and operating costs, the hourly rate cost component for repair costs can be established either from past records or by obtaining estimates from the equipment manufac-turer. In our example, we assume an hourly repair cost of $12 per hour. If the firm should rent the equipment, the vendor renting the equipment includes an hourly repair cost in the rental rate.

$$\text{Repair cost (operating cost)} = \$12/\text{hour}$$

Finance or interest cost

The purchase of equipment often entails a large expenditure, which, in our example, is $240,000. If the firm finances the equipment, the hourly rate should include a finance component. If the firm uses its own money to purchase the equipment, the loss of opportunity interest income should be reflected in the hourly rate for the equip-ment. Either way, the hourly cost includes a finance or interest cost component.

The finance or interest cost component can be a substantial hourly cost component. For example, assume an interest rate of 8 percent a year. Based on a purchase cost of $240,000, the annual interest expense would be $240,000 times 0.08 or $19,200. Given an estimated 1,000 hours of productive use in a given year, the hourly rate component for the finance or interest cost would be as follows:

$$\text{Finance or Interest Rate (ownership cost)} = \frac{\$19,200}{1,000 \text{ hours}} = \$19.20/\text{hour}$$

Note that we have referred to this hourly cost component as an "ownership cost" in that the cost depends on time only. It makes no difference if the equipment is being used or not; the residential builder would still incur the interest cost.

The above calculation of the finance or interest hourly cost should be viewed as an approximation. A more exact analysis would result in a somewhat lower hourly rate than the $19.20, owing to the fact that the finance cost would decrease as the principle on the loan was reduced.

Insurance cost

Given the substantial financial outlay for a piece of equipment, the owner of the equipment is likely to carry insurance on it. The calculation of the insurance hourly cost is fairly straightforward and certain. An insurance company will give a quote for the annual insurance premium for a piece of equipment; for example, $2,000 a year for our example $240,000 piece of equipment. Given an estimate of 1,000 hours of productive use in a given year, the insurance cost component is determined as follows:

$$\text{Insurance cost (ownership cost)} = \frac{\$2,000}{1,000 \text{ hours}} = \$2.00/\text{hour}$$

Property Tax cost

Some states require a residential builder to pay property taxes on owned equipment just like a property tax on real estate. If this is the case, the hourly property tax cost would be determined by dividing the annual property tax by the estimated hours of productive use in the year. Because few states charge property tax, we will assume this cost to be $0 in our example.

Replacement cost

Depreciation provides the firm a means of establishing a reserve to replace equipment when it is used up or obsolete. In effect, depreciation is a non-cash expense that is set off against profits to establish a savings account to hold funds to replace the equipment when the equipment is at the end of its life.

However, given inflation, equipment manufacturers annually increase the price of their equipment. The end result is that depreciation by itself will not be enough to replace the equipment. An inflation replacement cost component should also be included in the equipment hourly rate to replace the equipment at an inflated rate. For example, let us assume a 3 percent inflation rate in our example. This means that every year, the equipment would increase 3 percent in regards to buying a new similar machine. For our example, this would result in an increased purchase cost of $240,000 times 0.03 or $7,200 a year. The replacement cost component is determined as follows:

$$\text{Replacement cost (ownership cost)} = \frac{\$7{,}200}{1{,}000 \text{ hours}} = \$7.20/\text{hour}$$

If the construction cost does not include this replacement cost component in the hourly cost for the equipment, the firm is referred to as "going equipment poor," i.e. they are not building up a financial reserve to replace the equipment.

For the example equipment presented, the calculated hourly costs are shown in Figure 7-1.

For the example piece of equipment, the summary of the hourly costs is shown in Figure 7-2.

Why it is Important to View Equipment as Having an Operating Hourly Cost and an Ownership Hourly Cost?

The issue of equipment having costs that are a function of use (operating) and time (ownership), can affect the supervisor's managing of the equipment and project. The ability to improve equipment and

---

FIGURE 7-1 Hourly Costs for Example Piece of Equipment

Operating Costs (use related)			Ownership Costs (time related)		
Depreciation	=	$24.00	Depreciation*	=	$0
Maintenance	=	7.00	Finance or interest	=	$19.20
Operating	=	9.00	Insurance	=	2.00
Repair	=	12.00	Replacement	=	7.20
TOTAL	=	$52.00	TOTAL	=	$28.40

*We have listed depreciation in the above table under operating and ownership cost related (even though we have assumed in our example that the depreciation is a function of use only), because the value of equipment is a function of both time and use.

FIGURE 7-2 Summary of Hourly Costs for Example Piece of Equipment

Hourly cost (example equipment)	Costs	%
Operating Cost	$52.00	64.7
Ownership Cost	$28.40	35.3
Total Hourly Cost	$80.40	100

jobsite productivity is in part dependent on the supervisor's knowledge of productivity. Some issues affected by the knowledge of equipment costs include the following:

- Decisions to work overtime
- Issues as to when equipment should be kept or replaced
- Keeping equipment at a jobsite versus releasing it
- Change order costing

Decisions to work overtime

To the layperson, it would appear that roadway contractors work many weekend and long extended workdays. It is not unusual to observe a paving crew working late into the night.

Part of the reason the roadway contractor may work an extensive number of overtime hours relates to a tight project schedule, which may include a monetary bonus if the construction firm completes a project early. A second reason may relate to the issue that once a work activity such as placing asphalt starts, the construction firm may want to proceed until the work is complete.

However, another relevant issue relates to the roadway contractor's high dependence on equipment. An example roadway contractor estimate for an assumed $1 million roadway project is shown in Figure 7-3.

In the example project, equipment cost represents 40 percent of the overall bid. In many residential building projects, the equipment cost is less than 10 percent of the overall bid. If we assume that approximately 30 percent of the equipment costs in the above

FIGURE 7-3 Example of a Roadway Contractor Estimate		
Estimate Cost Component	**Costs**	**%**
On-site labor cost	$200,000	20
Material cost	150,000	15
Equipment cost	400,000	40
General conditions cost	100,000	10
Company overhead and profit	150,000	15
Total	**$1,000,000**	**100**

estimate is equipment ownership costs, then it follows that more than $100,000 of the equipment costs in the estimate are "time" related. If the contractor is or is not working on Saturday, these time-related costs continue to run. Given the high equipment costs, including the large ownership cost component (time related), it may be that the supervisor can afford to pay workers time and a half on a Saturday and still have a lower unit cost of production than if they did not work on Saturday and still incurred the equipment time related costs.

The point is that the decision to work overtime or not to work overtime is more complex when the work process is equipment-intensive. The supervisor has to make a calculation of the added premium labor rate (and labor inefficiency related to workers working overtime) relative to the benefit of "savings" related to the equipment ownership cost component.

Issues as to when equipment should be kept or replaced

One of the more difficult issues regarding equipment management relates to how long to keep or replace a piece of equipment. While the construction supervisor may not be directly involved in this decision, it does bring up issues that the supervisor should be aware of when managing equipment.

In the previous example regarding a piece of equipment, we calculated and used an equipment maintenance hourly rate, operating hourly rate, and repair hourly rate of $7, $9, and $12 respectively. In reality, these costs likely increase over time. For example, similar to an automobile, the annual repair costs for a piece of equipment increase over time. In fact, the increase is more than linear and may be represented by the curve shown in Figure 7-4.

While the maintenance cost and operating cost likely do not increase on an annual basis as dramatically as the repair cost illustrated, they do increase as a function of time. The operating costs tend to get more expensive over time; like an automobile, they tend to make it very expensive to keep owning and operating the equipment.

Another consideration relevant to the issue of retaining versus trading a piece of equipment relates to the equipment's **availability** factor or percentage. Depending on the type of equipment, the manufacturer of the equipment, the age of the equipment, and how well it is maintained, the availability percentage for equipment varies. For example, manufacturers of excavation equipment may suggest that, on average, their equipment is available 85 percent of the time for use in doing production work. During the other 15 percent of the time the equipment will be in service or possibly in a breakdown state. The availability factor or percent likely decreases as a function of time and as a function of the maintenance and repair costs. If a piece of equipment is not well maintained, it tends to break down more often and needs additional service time.

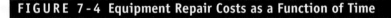

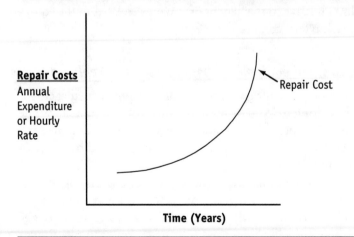

FIGURE 7-4 Equipment Repair Costs as a Function of Time

Repair Costs
Annual
Expenditure
or Hourly
Rate

Repair Cost

Time (Years)

If the availability time for a piece of equipment decreases, the construction supervisor is likely to incur an added cost-the cost of an idle crew of workers that is waiting on the availability of the equipment. A crew cost may be well in excess of $100, maybe even as much as $500. If the crew is dependent on the availability of a piece of equipment and the equipment should break down, the construction supervisor may incur this crew cost without any offsetting production; it is clearly a cost that jeopardizes the ability to complete a project on time and on budget.

This is one of the considerations a construction firm uses in deciding to use a preventive maintenance program. A preventive maintenance program essentially means that maintenance expenditures are made on a regular basis to a machine before the equipment breaks down. Records are kept as to when equipment parts should be changed relative to their typical life. While some added maintenance expenditures might be made using such a program, they likely are offset by the avoidance of the idle crew costs related to unexpected equipment breakdowns.

The point is that how well the supervisor maintains equipment, availability factors, preventive maintenance expenditures, and other issues make the managing of equipment and the issue of retaining versus trading a piece of equipment very complex. For example, Figure 7-5 might be representative of various considerations in the decision.

The complexity of the issue as to when is the best time to trade in a piece of equipment does not lessen the importance of the decision. For an equipment-intense construction firm, the decision as to when to trade in an old piece of equipment for a new one significantly affects the effective hourly cost of the equipment and the productivity and unit cost of doing work. Even if the supervisor does not make the decision as to when to trade in a piece of equipment, his or her actions as to how the equipment is used and maintained affect the decision.

The fact that there are several types of ownership and operating costs associated with using construction equipment also complicates the issue as to what type or brand of equipment the residential builder should purchase. While a piece of equipment from one manufacturer might have a higher initial cost (and therefore a higher depreciation hourly cost) than a similar piece of equipment from

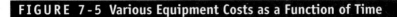

FIGURE 7-5 Various Equipment Costs as a Function of Time

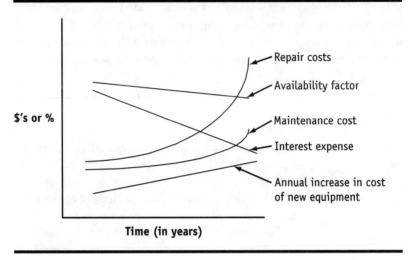

$'s or %

Repair costs

Availability factor

Maintenance cost

Interest expense

Annual increase in cost
of new equipment

Time (in years)

another manufacturer, it may have a lower repair, maintenance, and/or operating costs. In addition, the more expensive equipment (in regards to initial cost) may have a higher availability factor. Therefore, over a period of time, the more expensive equipment (initial cost) may have a lower **life cycle** cost. Clearly, the ability to understand equipment costs is fundamental to the managing of equipment to optimize productivity and lower unit cost of doing work.

Keeping equipment at a jobsite versus releasing it

It is fairly common to witness a construction supervisor who keeps equipment at a jobsite even though he or she may not immediately need the equipment. Rather than return the equipment to the company's main office, the supervisor takes the position that if it is returned to the main office, he or she may not get it back when needed. Therefore, the supervisor tends to hold the equipment at the jobsite in an idle or nonproductive state.

The problem with the above philosophy is twofold. For one, equipment is not "free" when sitting idle on a project. We have learned that at the very least, the residential builder is incurring ownership costs (i.e. finance costs) that are a function of time when a piece of equipment is in an idle or nonproductive state. Secondly, when the supervisor ties up the equipment at one jobsite, it may be at the expense of another company supervisor who needs the equipment at another jobsite. It may be that the supervisor has the equipment in an idle or standby state at his or her job, only to find out that another supervisor lost productivity because of the unavailability of the equipment.

The supervisor's decision as to when to hold versus when to release a piece of equipment needs to consider the operations of the entire firm, not just his or her project. In order to optimize firm productivity and profits, equipment decisions need to be made on a larger scale than when deciding on the actions to take with a specific worker on a project.

Given the above concerns, the residential builder may implement a system of charging a supervisor two different rates—a productive and a standby rate—for the use of equipment. Such a system has the objective of making the supervisor aware of the fact that equipment is not free, even when it is standing idle.

To illustrate the system of charging a supervisor's job cost for productive and standby equipment time, let us assume that a residential builder captures the total costs associated with owning a specific piece of equipment in a single year to be $160,000. Assume that this $160,000 includes all the ownership and operating costs incurred in a year to include depreciation costs, maintenance and operating costs, etc.

Furthermore, let us assume that the residential builder budgets the piece of equipment in question as follows for the upcoming year:

$$\text{Budgeted productive hours} = 1{,}100 \text{ hours}$$
$$\text{Standby or nonproductive hours} = 900 \text{ hours}$$

Let us assume that the supervisor is to be charged two different hourly rates for the use of the equipment in question: X for productive hours and Y for standby or nonproductive hours.

Given annual equipment expenditures of $160,000, the following equation can be used to determine a means of charging all equipment expenditures to projects for the upcoming year.

(1,100 productive hours) $\times$ (Productive Hourly Rate – X)
+ (900 standby or nonproductive hours)
$\times$ (Standby or Nonproductive – Y) must
= $160,000

The residential builder can decide upon the productive rate X and the standby or nonproductive rate Y. However, once they decide on one rate, the other is determined from the equation. Let us assume in the example above that the firm decides upon a productive rate (X) of $100 per hour. The standby or nonproductive rate would then be $55.55. This is calculated below:

Budget annual equipment expenditures	$160,000
Minus budgeted productive equipment time =	
(1,100 hrs) x ($100/hr)	$110,000
Equals	50,000
Divided by budgeted standby or	
nonproductive hours =	900 hours
Equals Standby or nonproductive hourly rate =	$55.55

Using this system, the supervisor would be charged $100 per hour when he or she was using the equipment for productive operations. When the supervisor was holding the equipment in a standby or nonproductive state, his or her job-control report would be charged $55.55 per hour. In this case, the supervisor would pay somewhat of a penalty for holding equipment. That is not to say that there are not situations when a supervisor should hold a piece of equipment on standby. However, at least now, he or she would be accountable for productive and standby or nonproductive equipment time. The process defeats the position that equipment is free. The supervisor can now make a more quantitative analysis of when to hold equipment up and when to free it up. The system also reflects the sound accounting principle that accountability forces responsibility which in turn enables productivity.

Why did we use the $100 rate for the productive time and therefore end up with a standby rate or nonproductive rate of $55.55? The rates selected can be whatever the residential builder deems appropriate. As a guide, one might take the position that the standby or nonproductive rate should relate to the calculated "ownership rate"—the costs that are a function of time. This position is consistent with the principle that even when the equipment is standing idle, it is costing the firm an ownership rate.

The firm might also take the position that supervisors are holding up equipment too often. If this is true, the residential builder might actually adopt a standby or nonproductive equipment rate that is higher than the productive rate. Such a costing process would give the supervisor incentive to get equipment off their jobs when not needed for production.

By using different hourly rates for productive and standby or nonproductive time, the supervisor and the firm are likely to be more attentive to keeping equipment productive, which by itself is a worthy objective. A more sophisticated equipment-tracking system may actually charge the supervisor three different equipment rates— one for productive work, one for meaningful or justified standby time, and one for nonproductive time.

8

Managing Subcontractors

In residential construction, the majority of projects are constructed using several specialty firms, typically the residential builder and several subcontractors. While there are several different organizational structures to projects, including the design-build process and the construction management (CM) process, the organizational structure illustrated in Figure 8-1 remains the most common.

The subcontractors in Figure 8-1 are typically specialty firms and are commonly referred to as trade contractors. For a residential project, the subcontractors include the electrical, mechanical, and plumbing contractors.

In many cases, the residential builder illustrated in Figure 8-1 may do less than 30 percent of the overall construction work with their own workers. Sometimes, the residential builder may subcontract all the work.

The Need to Manage Subcontractors Without Being Able to Direct the Subcontractor

The supervisor working for the residential builder must manage his or her own self-performed work and coordinate and supervise the work of the subcontractors. The project performance, to include the project time, budget, quality, and safety, is only as good as its weakest link.

FIGURE 8-1 Typical Project Organizational Structure

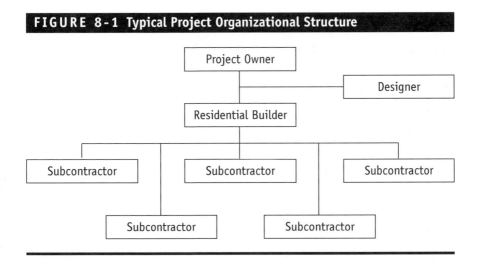

The role of the residential builder differs in regard to managing his or her own self-performed work versus the work of the subcontractors. In the case of self-performed work, the supervisor can "direct" his or her own workers. He or she determines how many workers to employ, assigns them work tasks, directs their work efforts, and monitors their production efforts.

In the case of the work performed by subcontractors, the role of the residential builder supervisor is less direct. The supervisor does not hire individual craftspersons for the subcontractors, estimate their production goals, or assign individual workers or crews to work tasks, and has little ability to reprimand or monitor individual worker and crew performance. In regard to subcontractor performance, the residential builder supervisor is in the delicate role of obtaining performance without having the right to "direct" performance. However, the supervisor cannot merely standby and watch the performance of the subcontractors; such an approach often leads to project difficulties. The supervisor must be proactive in his or her approach to subcontractors; the supervisor has to manage rather than watch their performance.

One often hears the builder or supervisor say, "We do a good job of project management and managing productivity. However, we cannot get our subcontractors to perform." This approach is one of blaming the other guy. Whether or not the blame is appropriate, the fact remains that the project is only as good as its weakest link. Any one builder's performance at a project typically affects the other contractors at the project. If subcontractors are in trouble in regard to their budgeted project time or cost, the general contractor will likely also be trouble.

The dilemma the supervisor faces is how to get subcontractors to perform without having direct control over their production process. The following practices are recommended

- Be more selective in hiring subcontractors
- Force the subcontractors to manage themselves
- Implement performance management procedures
- Implement accurate and timely accounting and reporting procedures
- Implement a team approach to project management
- Serve as an adviser and aid to the subcontractor

The Importance of Hiring the Right Subcontractors

The best way to manage subcontractors is to engage the right subcontractors so that they don't have to be managed. This is easier said than done!

The construction process is such that a premium is given to the lowest bidding contractor; more often than not the low-bidding subcontractor is contracted. However, a project is only successful if four variables are managed:

1. Project time
2. Project cost or budget
3. Project quality
4. Project safety

A subcontractor might be the low bidder and be contracted, only to demonstrate the following characteristics:

- Under-staff the project
- Be uncooperative in attending project meetings
- Be lackadaisical in regard to planning and scheduling work
- Be argumentative with other project contractors

- Do marginal quality of work
- Ignore project safety requirements

Any one of the above unfavorable characteristics is likely to lead to low productivity and overall project problems for everyone. While the residential builder and his or her supervisor may have contract clauses that enable them to come down on a subcontractor for any of the above problems, or even to terminate the subcontractor, this is not a solution, at best it is a remedy.

Evaluation of Subcontractor Performance

The following process for engaging subcontractors is recommended

1. Design a subcontractor evaluation form for evaluating subcontractor project performance.
2. During and after project completion, the supervisor should be required to evaluate each subcontractor's performance using the designed form.
3. A database should be established that rates subcontractor performance using the completed supervisor evaluation forms.
4. The database of past performance should be utilized for evaluating and selecting subcontractors for future projects.

Given the fact that the project owner typically engages the residential builder in a low bid environment, it is obvious that the residential builder must also seek competitive bids from subcontractors. However, if a low bidding subcontractor fails to perform productively, the residential builder and the supervisor will likely incur problems that may be more severe than not having been the successful bidder on the project.

Helping Subcontractors Help Themselves

The supervisor often attempts to manage the subcontractor by taking a results-oriented approach. The supervisor gets the subcontractor to promise results, such as a completion date, and then comes down on the subcontractor when the results are not achieved. This approach typically results in finger pointing, assessing blame, disputes, and possibly lawsuits.

A more positive approach, and an approach that is more likely to achieve results, is to force the subcontractor to manage his or her own construction process via the use of various management practices. This is compatible with the principle that if you fix the process, the results will take care of themselves.

An example of a subcontractor helping himself is the issue of formalized project scheduling, which supervisors often have difficulty getting their subcontractors to do. Project planning and scheduling was covered in an earlier chapter. It was pointed out that formalized on-paper planning and scheduling improves productivity by setting out milestone dates, drawing attention to resources needed to do the work, and by providing a means of measuring and monitoring performance. Formalized planning and scheduling is just as important for an electrical, mechanical, or plumbing contractor as it is for the residential builder.

Instead of complaining about the subcontractor who does not prepare adequate, formalized planning and scheduling, the residential builder can require the subcontractor to do so in the contract. It can be just as much of a contract requirement as putting in electrical conduit. When the subcontractor agrees in his or her contract to do formalized planning and scheduling, the supervisor should then enforce it. Leaving a subcontractor off the hook when it comes to scheduling commitments will not do the subcontractor or the residential builder a favor.

While the supervisor cannot "direct" or force the subcontractor to do things that they have not agreed to in the contract, the supervisor does have the right to enforce what the subcontractor has agreed to do. The key is to get the subcontractor to commit to defined management practices in the contract and then enforce the commitments. In effect, the supervisor is forcing the subcontractor to manage him or herself.

Implementing Performance Management for Subcontractors

One of the problems the supervisor has when it comes to managing subcontractors is getting them to meet their schedule commitments. This often stems from the fact that subcontractors have the same problem the residential builder has: they have more work to do, or more projects to do, than they have resources to do the work.

Getting the subcontractor to commit to a start date and an end date for the work is not enough. Effective subcontractor management entails the following:

- Getting subcontractors to break down their work into a detailed list of work activities.
- Getting subcontractors to set out various milestone dates as well as the end date.
- Getting subcontractors to commit to how they are going to do work activities as well as when they are going to complete them; in other words, getting them to commit to effort, not just results.

1. Requiring subcontractors to break down their schedule into more detail

When reviewing a formalized on-paper schedule for a project, it is common to observe that the residential builder has broken down his or her work into many individual work activities; often one hundred or more detailed work activities. Then, one observes that the subcontractor's portion of the work is often much less detailed. For example, there may be one single work activity, such as "Put in Plumbing—14 weeks," to represent the entire plumbing effort.

Requiring a subcontractor to submit a schedule and then accepting a schedule that does not break down the work in detail does not do the subcontractor or the builder a favor. If a subcontractor submits a schedule with one work activity-put in plumbing—14 weeks-then the first time nonperformance can be identified is after the 14 weeks is over. The schedule becomes a tool for assessing blame rather than a tool for getting things done.

In setting out the subcontractors' scheduling requirements, the following should be considered:

- Specify the minimum number of work activities the subcontractor must set out in the schedule he or she submits.

- Give guidelines as to the format of the schedule; for example, activities on the first floor are to be separate from activities on the second floor, or activities are to be shown by room location.
- Consider requiring that the duration of any one work activity can be no larger than a defined duration, for example, 10 days. This will force the subcontractor to break down the work into more detail.

The principle behind requiring the subcontractor to break down his or her work into more detail on the schedule is that is forces him or her to think through the work process. The mere fact that the work is broken down into more detail will force the subcontractor to think through resource conflicts and construction problems. This in itself should enhance project productivity.

2. Setting out milestone dates

The last resort to subcontractor management is terminating them for nonperformance. While this is a last-resort management action, it does not even become a feasible alternative when the supervisor merely gets the subcontractor to promise a completion date. If this is all the subcontractor has promised, the supervisor has a difficult time reprimanding the subcontractor for a lack of effort or for improperly manning the project until the promised date is missed. This is illustrated in Figure 8-2.

A more effective means of managing the subcontractor entails getting the subcontractor to commit to various milestone dates. By doing so, the supervisor has the ability to reprimand the subcontractor more quickly and corrective actions can be taken. Given a desperate situation, the supervisor may even consider terminating the subcontractor. The positive purpose of the milestone dates illustrated in Figure 8-2 is to get the subcontractor's attention as to how he or she is going to get work completed to meet milestone dates. Without the milestone date commitments the subcontractor might procrastinate until it is too late to meet the project completion date.

FIGURE 8-2 Milestone Scheduling

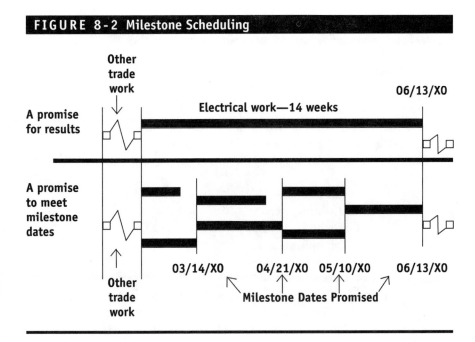

3. Commitment for effort, not just results

Like most businesses, the subcontractor may be overcommitted and have limited resources. The supervisor cannot afford to be on the bottom of the totem pole when it comes to getting the subcontractor's attention, effort, and resources.

With the dual objective of 1) getting the subcontractor to plan out how he or she is going to get work done and 2) getting a formalized commitment to make the appropriate effort to staff his or her work, the supervisor can require the subcontractor to provide a resource-loaded schedule. The resource-loaded schedule not only sets out work activity durations and milestone dates, but also requires the subcontractor to set out the resources they will use for performing each work activity. For example, if one of the work activities in Figure 9-2 is to put in 20,000 linear feet of 3/4-inch electrical conduit, the subcontractor might show this work taking 10 days. To get the work done in 10 days, the subcontractor has had to consider the following three pieces of information:

- Productivity of a worker putting in 3/4-inch electrical conduit
- Production delays that may occur, such as weather
- Number of electricians or crew size that will be used to do the work

For example, using a productivity of 20 linear feet per craft-hour, 1,000 craft-hours will be required. Assuming one day of work disruption (leaving nine), the electrical subcontractor will have to have the following number of workers doing the work:

Work days available	= 9 days
Craft-hours needed	= 1,000
Craft-hours needed per day =	111
Work hours per day	= 8
Number of workers needed =	14

By getting the subcontractor to work through the above calculations and indicate 14 workers for the work activity, the supervisor accomplishes the two objectives of 1) getting the subcontractor to plan the work and think through how many workers he or she needs for each work task and 2) in effect committing the subcontractor to having 14 workers present.

Having had the subcontractor commit to the 14 workers, the supervisor can now monitor the subcontractor's effort, not just the results. This is not to say that the supervisor should go ballistic every time the subcontractor is short one worker. However, the mere fact that the subcontractor knows that he or she has committed to 14 workers will more likely keep him or her more conscious of having the 14 workers doing the work. A promise for effort, not just results, gives the supervisor much more control in regard to recognizing potential project delays.

Getting the Subcontractor to Plan Tomorrow's Work Today

One of the main causes for waiting and nonproductive time at projects relates to workers and their supervisors looking for things or waiting for things that should have been lined up the day before. Workers waiting on materials, a crew waiting on a tool that cannot be located, or not having the right equipment at the project when needed are all examples of events that negatively impact overall project productivity.

Employees of the residential builder as well as employees of subcontractors fall victim to the failure to plan tomorrow's work today. In an early unit, a short interval scheduling form was presented for use by supervisors to remind them to line up materials, tools, equipment, and labor that is going to be needed the following day. The same form required the supervisor to set out a production goal for each work activity they were going to perform the following day.

Recognizing that subcontractor work delays negatively impact the subcontractor's performance as well as the overall project, the supervisor should consider requiring the subcontractors to use the same short interval scheduling form noted in the earlier unit. One way to do this is for the supervisor to provide the subcontractors with the form similar to the one shown in Figure 8-3 and require the subcontractors to submit the completed form on a daily basis.

FIGURE 8-3 Form for Subcontractor Daily Planning Input

Short Interval Scheduling Form

Project: _____   Foreman: _____

Plan for Day: _____   Supervisor: _____

Work Activity Planned	Quantity Goal	# Workers (Crew) Required	Material Required	Equipment Required	Tools Required	Notes

The intent is to force the subcontractors to do what they should do anyway-plan tomorrow's work today. Will the subcontractors submit to the residential builder supervisor? The answer to this depends on how persistent the supervisor is in his or her request. If the subcontractor is advised of this requirement as a basis of his or her contract, the subcontractor will likely do whatever is required of them. It is the supervisor's role to enforce the process just like it is his or her role to require the subcontractors to perform work according to the specifications. The alternative is to stand by and watch nonproductive waiting time and to point blame at firms for their failure to get things done. A proactive approach focuses on improving the process to get results.

In addition to the form shown in Figure 8-3, the supervisor could require the subcontractor to report on what they did finish on a given day relative to the budgeted quantities made the day before using the form shown. The intent is to hold the subcontractor accountable for meeting production goals.

There are additional procedures aimed at project management that the supervisor might impose on the subcontractors. If the procedures aid in increasing productivity, their implementation will help the project and the individual subcontractors meet their goals.

Productivity Through Accountability and Record Keeping

Accountability tends to make people responsible, which in turn make them more productive. In his or her effort to manage subcontractors and attain favorable jobsite productivity, the supervisor must keep extensive daily records of who did what and when.

It is important that the supervisor keep daily records regarding both subcontractor performance and the supervisor's own self-performed work. While the types of information recorded on a daily basis may differ, the objective is the same-to be able to play the project events back like a movie after the fact.

Record Keeping and Subcontractor Performance

Daily record keeping serves several purposes, including providing a basis of proving right or wrong when a dispute evolves and as input for additional management reports like project status reports. However, one of the main purposes of record keeping is to identify who did what and when. There is a strong relationship between accountability and productivity. Holding individuals and firms responsible increases the probability that they will perform and owe up to their responsibilities, which, in turn, promotes productivity.

The form used to track daily subcontractor performance will vary from firm to firm. However, at a minimum, the supervisor needs to record the following information daily regarding subcontractor performance:

- Number of workers
- Supervisors present
- Equipment present
- Equipment used
- Type of work performed
- Materials delivered
- Instructions given
- Instructions asked
- Construction method difficulties
- Productivity difficulties
- Safety issues
- Quality of work issues
- Conformance with contract administration requirements
- Attendance at meetings
- Compliance with scheduling requirements

The above list is not meant to be all-inclusive. Given the unique characteristics of each project and the type of work each subcontractor performs, reporting requirements for the supervisor regarding subcontractor performance need to be reviewed and revised.

The point is that it is important for subcontractors to know they are being monitored and evaluated as the project work progresses. The mere fact that they know they will be held accountable will enhance their attention to performance.

Positive Communication with Subcontractors

Failure to communicate correctly and in a timely manner is a leading cause of low productivity in the construction industry. The construction process is characterized by slow or inaccurate jobsite record keeping, by different individuals and firms having different objectives and intentionally or unintentionally withholding information, and by a job-control process that is weekly or monthly, a time frame that makes it too late to correct productivity problems effectively.

Many of the onsite production problems that occur at jobsites could be lessened or eliminated if only the problems would have been identified earlier and communicated to individuals who could address the issues. Many of the construction disputes and lawsuits that are part of the construction industry could be avoided if individuals or firms would simply communicate the problem, identify the cause of the problem, and remedy the situation. Instead, small problems tend to grow into large monetary problems, which eventually will negatively impact the project's time, budget, quality, and safety objectives.

Effective communication is more of a skill or an art than it is a science. As discussed in an earlier chapter on personnel management, effective communication is an essential component to keeping workers productive. It is equally important that the supervisor be attentive to timely and effective communication with subcontractors. The following practices should be implemented into communications with subcontractors:

- Don't procrastinate. Most construction productivity problems become bigger problems if they are not communicated and addressed.
- Try to use positive communication. Spend as much time commending the subcontractor's good efforts as you do blaming them for poor efforts.
- Remember that effective communication entails both talking and listening. Make an effort to listen to subcontractors; ask them for their ideas to solve problems.
- n communicating with subcontractors, try to create ideas and solutions that are a win-win situation for both the subcontractors and the residential builder. If the subcontractors believe everything they are being asked to do only benefits the residential builder or you as the supervisor, they likely will not align to your recommendations or instructions.

- Keep channels of communication open with all subcontractors. Encourage subcontractors to communicate their concerns and problems.
- When giving instructions to a subcontractor, always try to explain why you are giving the instructions and the benefits that will be achieved if the instructions are followed.
- Try to act as an adviser to your subcontractors, not just a director.
- Set up a process for communicating success as well as failure.
- Understand your subcontractors. Some need more instruction, some need encouragement, and some need reprimanding. Different people and different firms have different needs and knowledge.
- Consider new signage at jobsites that communicates job status, successes, and recognition.

Holding Productive Meetings

Holding formalized jobsite meetings is part of the communication system at a construction site. Given the complexity of the construction process and the many different firms and subcontractors that are dependent upon one another in the work process, an essential component of a productivity improvement program is job meetings.

Meetings can be categorized as one of four types:

1. Reporting and information
2. Problem solving
3. Brainstorming for improvement
4. Educational and training

Reporting and information meetings are typically scheduled for a set time and place. Weekly jobsite meetings to discuss project status, project schedules, and safety are examples of reporting and information meetings. The meeting has the objective of communicating information to all subcontractors. They should be encouraged to attend.

Problem solving meetings can be viewed as more of an emergency type of meeting. The meeting should be scheduled as soon as a significant problem arises. A construction failure in a work method, an accident, and the recognition of a significant cost overrun should each initiate a meeting with all entities that caused the problem, can solve the problem, and/or are affected by the problem. The supervisor should use problem solving techniques such as data analysis to facilitate these meetings.

Brainstorming for improvement meetings can be combined with one of the above two types of meetings or held independent of them. The purpose is to challenge current practices, to think "out of the box," to find a better way to do things. Supervisors seldom hold this type of meeting with project subcontractors, but holding them on a random or scheduled basis actually may reduce the need for problem solving meetings. The mood and productivity at a project will be more positive if new improvement ideas can be uncovered at a brainstorming meeting as opposed to spending the majority of the time pointing fingers at problem solving meetings.

The resistance to holding brainstorming meetings likely stems from the fact that there is no guarantee that the meeting will yield results. However, given the potential that exists in the construction process, there often is a favorable benefit cost ratio associated with the brainstorming meeting. In addition, such a meeting has the potential to draw out subcontractor creativity and improvement.

Educational or training meetings have the objective of providing information to enable workers and firms to be more productive. Training entails giving individuals information that is likely to yield benefits or improvement quickly. On the other hand, education is giving individuals information with the intent of obtaining benefits over a longer time frame.

Training and education have not historically been major priorities of residential builders. On occasion, residential builders hold in-house training or educational sessions or seminars. However, they seldom are offered or given on a project basis. When one considers the fact that a project fails at the weakest link, the supervisor should consider offering training or education on a project basis, especially if the project is complex and requires the cooperation and knowledge of all entities, including project subcontractors. For example, instead of complaining about subcontractors not knowing or using formalized scheduling, the supervisor might weigh the benefits of providing them with scheduling training or education.

Independent of the type of meeting held, the purpose is one of communication. The meeting should be productive. The meeting agenda should be well defined and communicated to all subcontractors prior to the meeting, and it should be structured so that all parties have an opportunity to contribute input. However, the meeting should not be allowed to drift to nonproductive chitchat or turn into a name-calling, negative environment. Meetings can be an effective tool for integrating subcontractors into a team if the supervisor promotes a positive, improvement-focused atmosphere.

Team Building with Subcontractors

The very nature of the construction industry results in firms, supervisors, and craftspeople working for "jobs" as opposed to "firms." The average construction project takes only a year or two to construct, if not less. Many individuals and firms go from job to job and may only work with one another on a single project. The end result is that individuals and firms may have a shortsighted view and take the position of "What's in it for me?"

The fact that subcontractors may only be working with a supervisor on one or a few projects makes it even more important that the supervisor be attentive to taking a team approach. There are too many ways one contractor on a project can negatively impact another contractor if they are not working toward a common goal. On the majority of construction projects, if one contractor, be it the general contractor or a subcontractor, is in trouble, then the others are probably in trouble. Time, cost, quality, and safety problems on a project tend to ripple to everyone.

Developing a team approach to project and subcontractor management is easier said than done when there is such a large emphasis on low cost and profits. The supervisor needs to be creative in coming up with ideas and procedures on how to have all individuals work as a team. Team building ideas include:

- Recognition and awards for all team accomplishments rather than individual accomplishments.
- Developing a win-win environment where one firm's success is not at the expense of another's loss.

- Implementing a quick problem resolution system so that problems cannot grow to the point that they prove divisive.
- Taking a forward approach to problem solving by identifying potential problems that may occur and agreeing to methods and means of problem resolution prior to them.

Partnering and dispute resolution boards are recent processes that the construction industry is using to develop a better team approach to construction. In partnering, all entities meet prior to the start of the project and agree to a series of common project goals and also decide how problems will be addressed if they do occur. In the dispute resolution process, one or three individuals are engaged as independent parties to quickly resolve problems or issues that come up during the construction process. Productivity improvement can best be achieved when everyone is pulling in the same direction!

9

Managing Change Orders and Disputes

Construction work performed by the residential builder can be classified as one of two types: base bid work and change order work. Base bid work is the work that was anticipated by the residential builder when the firm prepares its estimate and signs a contract. Change order work is extra work, work that was not anticipated. When a project owner or the designer representative recognizes a need for a change order and directs the residential builder to do the work, the change order is referred to as a "directed change." However, sometimes conditions change that result in what is referred to as a "constructive change." For example, if the project schedule changes, causing the firm to do the work in a colder environment, which in turn impacts the firm's productivity, it can be argued that the firm has been subjected to a constructive change.

Change orders often prove troublesome in regard to determining the impact they have on project time, cost, and overall labor and equipment productivity. Because the project owner and the residential builder may not be able to agree on the cause of the change order or the impact on project cost or project time, it follows that change orders are one of the leading reasons for construction disputes, claims, and lawsuits.

Change Order Process

Change orders or changed work can result from many causes. Some of the reasons for a change order include the following:

- Project owner changes his or her mind about a project component or design
- Designer omitted something or made an error
- Code changes that require a design change
- Working conditions change, such as a long delay because of weather
- Unknown project conditions, such as unrepresentative soil conditions
- Construction performance difficulties; non-constructible design

There are other causes, some of which are unique to the project.

Independent of the cause of a change order, when a change order occurs three different forms typically accompany it. The typical process is illustrated in Figure 9-1.

Unfortunately, the change order process often does not flow as ideally as shown in Figure 9-1. Problems occur that make the change order process complex and cause various issues. A list of some of the problems, issues that occur, and supervisor recommendations are noted in Figure 9-2.

FIGURE 9-1 The Change Order Paper Flow

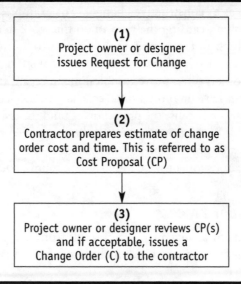

FIGURE 9-2 Problems, Issues, and Supervisor Recommendations for COS

Problem	Issue	Supervisor Recommendation
No step 1. Contractor says work is added, i.e. wants CO and project owner says that it is base bid work.	Project owner will not recognize change order request.	Do work under protest. Document everything.
Contractor puts together CP, but project owner disagrees with the dollar amount or time requested.	The contractor is being requested to proceed with work without having agreed to a dollar amount for the work.	Ideally, the supervisor should require a written agreement to the scope of work, dollar amount to be paid, and time required to do the work. Lacking any of these, the supervisor should document everything as work proceeds.
Project owner does not react to every CP in a timely manner; instead, the project owner issues a single CO for several CPs.	Contractor is being requested to proceed with CP work without an agreement. In addition, there can be a considerable time lag between when work is performed and when contractor receives payment.	Supervisor should attempt to pressure project owner to issue COs more timely. If COs are not issued timely, the supervisor should quantify a request for the loss of the time value of money associated with late payment.
The change work is such that the amount of work cannot be determined until the work is complete.	This makes it difficult if not impossible for the contractor and the project owner to agree to a dollar amount or time required to do the work prior to starting the work.	The supervisor requires an agreement as to "how" the work is to be paid; for example, a time and material agreement.
The change order work is substantial and causes a productivity impact to base bid work that affects the overall project cost and overall project schedule.	This effect on other work and overall project schedule is often referred to as "impact." The project owner may be unwilling to recognize the impact.	Supervisor should make an effort to quantify the impact of changes on base bid (see later section in this chapter).

(*Continued*)

FIGURE 9-2 Problems, Issues, and Supervisor Recommendations for COS (*Continued*)

Problem	Issue	Supervisor Recommendation
Not all change orders involve added work. The contractor also can request a change for added project time owing to events that occur; failure of designer to respond to requests for information (RFIs).	The project owner and contractor may not agree to the issues causing the time extension, the amount of time requested, or the financial impact associated with the time extension.	Supervisor should use formalized scheduling techniques to document time impacts.

It should be noted that many unique problems and issues evolve on specific projects. Therefore, the supervisor recommendations set out in Figure 9-2 need to be modified for each situation. In some cases, the supervisor needs to discuss the situation with the home office and there may be a need to consult legal counsel as to what action to take.

Excusable and Compensatory Delays

When a change order occurs, it upsets the rhythm of the project; often negatively impacting project time and cost. In addition to diluting the ratio of supervision of working craftsmen and disrupting the sequencing of the project, the change may result in project delays. When the project completion is delayed, both the project owner and residential builder may incur added costs. For one, the project owner may incur a loss of revenue. Therefore, they often impose a liquidated damage clause in the contract that is enforced against the residential builder. A project delay also impacts the residential builder. At the very minimum, the residential builder incurs additional costs associated with added general condition costs such as supervision costs and onsite utilities.

Change orders often result in project delays. Project delays often are caused by one of the following three reasons:

1. Caused by or within the control of the project owner or their designer
2. Caused by or within the control of the residential builder
3. Caused by events outside the control of the project owner and residential builder

Regardless of the cause of the delay, it is important to differentiate between a delay that affects an activity on the critical path of the project schedule and an activity that is not on the critical path. The activities on the critical path establish the overall project duration. If a critical path activity is impacted by a delay, it almost always results in a project time extension. The question is, does the cause of the delay entitle the residential builder to a time extension or not? This is an important issue because if the residential builder is not entitled to extended time, the firm will likely be responsible for liquidated damages associated with an extended project time. If the residential builder is entitled to a time extension (and therefore relieved of the liquidated damages), the delay is referred to as excusable. If the residential builder is not entitled to a time extension, the delay is referred to as being nonexcusable.

A second question is, even if the residential builder is entitled to a time extension (i.e. excusable), is the firm entitled to compensation for the added extended general condition costs? If the residential builder is not entitled to the extended time related financial damages, the damages are referred to as being non-compensatory.

If the reason for the delay is caused by or within the control of the project owner, the residential builder usually is entitled to both a time extension and the extended general condition costs. This type of delay is excusable and compensatory.

At the other extreme is a delay caused by or within the control of the residential builder. This type of delay is nonexcusable and non-compensatory. The firm is not entitled to a time extension (and therefore is assessed liquidated damages), and is not entitled to reimbursement for added general conditions.

The most difficult resolution relates changes and the associated time delay for events outside the control of both the project owner and the residential builder. An example would be the change of a city code in the middle of a project that caused the project to be extended. Each situation is somewhat unique and the case must be resolved on its own merit. However, there is some precedence for awarding the residential builder an extension of time for these types of delays, but no financial damages for extended general conditions. The end result is that this type of delay is excusable and non-compensatory.

The three types of delays and their resolutions (assuming they impact the critical path and the project duration) are illustrated in Figure 9-3.

A directed change order is a change order issued by the project owner for additional work. A constructive change order is when the residential builder does base bid work and the productivity is negatively impacted by factors outside his or her control and responsibility. Directed changes are almost always considered excusable and compensatory to the contractor. However, a constructive change order has to be judged on the unique issues of the cause and the result.

Concurrent delays

Sometimes multiple delays occur at the same time during a project. The question becomes one of determining what period of time is

FIGURE 9-3 Types of Delays and Their Resolutions

Type of delay or change	Examples	Result
Excusable and compensatory	Owner-directed change orders Change in site conditions Late delivery of owner supplied material	Contractor entitled to project time extension (no liquidated damages) and general condition financial damages
Excusable and noncompensatory	Prior contractor late Code change	Contractor entitled to project time extension but no general condition financial damages
Non-Excusable and non-compensatory	Adverse but expected bad weather Construction method failure or collapse	Contractor not entitled to project time extension nor general condition financial damages

excusable and what period of time is compensatory. In other words, how many days of time is the residential builder entitled to for time extensions, and how many days can be used in the calculation of compensatory damages for extended general conditions? Each of these somewhat complex situations has to be evaluated based on the issues.

Overriding contract clauses

The residential builder should be cautioned that agreed-to contract language may be such that the results discussed above as to which delays are excusable and compensatory may be different. Examples of these clauses include the following:

No damage for delay clause

This contract clause typically provides that in the event of any delay, the sole remedy for the contractor is an extension of time, but no extended general condition costs.

Force majeure clause

A force majeure clause allocates the risks for delays caused by events that are beyond the control of the project owner/designer and contractor. For example, the clause may limit the contractor to a request for time but not additional general condition financial damages for owner-directed changes. Normally, a contractor would request time and general condition costs for this type of change order. Clearly it is important for the residential builder to read the contract documents, especially the supplementary conditions, to ensure they know the unique contract language.

Construction Claim

When a change order dispute (for example, the project owner and contractor cannot agree on the scope of work or dollar amount), the dispute may become a claim.

A construction claim can be defined as the following:

> *"A construction claim is a request for additional compensation by a contractor for added work they allege to have performed or for*

added costs associated with doing base bid work under conditions they did not expect and are not responsible for incurring."

Claims can become a time-consuming and costly part of many construction projects. Cost records and documentation of events can prevent a dispute and therefore a claim. This is the best possible claim for two entities-the best claim is the one that doesn't evolve. While the prevention of claims is the cure-all for many of the woes of the construction industry, the reality is that claims often take place. It is at this point in time that the ability to properly prepare a claim becomes a critical process for the damaged entity.

Two issues evolve when a dispute or claim arises:

1. Entitlement
2. The quantum or financial damages

The entitlement issue regarding a dispute relates to who is right and who is wrong and it often becomes a legal issue. The facts of each dispute or claim are unique and the supervisor has to keep good records and documentation.

The quantum or financial damages associated with disputes and claims typically include several categories, such as added material costs, added equipment costs, general condition costs, and allocation of company overhead.

A construction dispute or claim typically includes a substantial onsite labor cost component. The labor cost component in turn consists of two components or types. First, there is an issue of direct labor cost. For example, if the contractor has to do extra work because of a change order, there is the issue of how many additional labor hours and labor costs were incurred. This may be complicated by the fact that the labor hours are not well segmented from other work the firm performs. The key, therefore, is for the supervisor to do a detailed listing and segmenting of the labor hours and costs of added or disputed work.

The second type of labor hours or costs is often more complex. This relates to more of a cause-and-effect issue. The supervisor can use several different methods to quantify the lost labor productivity owing to changes.

Methods of Quantifying Lost Labor Productivity

1. Discrete Method

In the Discrete Method, construction personnel on the jobsite attempt to record alleged productivity inefficiencies directly onto the daily time card or daily report. "Impact" codes are created and lost time is recorded as shown in Figure 9-4.

This is often viewed as the best approach because the lost hours are identified and segmented on the timecard. But, in reality, this method seldom is used. For one, experience has shown that many supervisors don't get serious about a problem until the project it is near the end or over, and this prevents them from recognizing the hours on the timecard as they occur. Secondly, timecards are traditionally used to record labor hours against the budgeted hours. Because defects or time delays are not part of the budget, they normally are not recorded on the timecard.

2. Measured Mile Approach

In this method, the productivity achieved during the alleged troublesome period is compared to the productivity achieved

FIGURE 9-4 Example Timecard

DAILY TIMECARD	
Description	**Hours**
Erect slab forms	2.0
Place rebar	2.5
Place concrete in slab	2.5
Waiting on materials	0.5
Waiting on drawings	0.5
Total	**8.0**

when there was not trouble or impact. This approach is illustrated in Figure 9-5.

The Measured Mile presents a graphical or mathematical means of illustrating alleged lost labor productivity. This method assumes that the work performed in the non-impact periods and the work performed in the alleged impact period was similar.

The measured mile exhibit can be prepared as the claim issue evolves or can be prepared from past records.

3. Total Cost Method

In this method, the alleged labor productivity cost damage is calculated as the difference between the actual project labor cost and the estimated labor cost or hours. An example is illustrated in Figure 9-6.

In effect, the Total Cost Method assumes the following:

1. That the estimating process was correct and that the resulting estimated hours and cost amount are correct.
2. That the recorded project labor cost and hours are correct.
3. That all the reasons for the overrun in the labor cost damage are the fault of the project owner or designer.
4. That the labor rate used in the calculation is a fair and equitable rate and represents what the contractor paid.

FIGURE 9-5 Measured Mile Approach

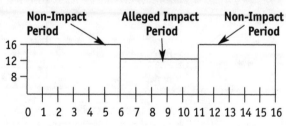

Calculation of Alleged Lost Productivity Impact

Assume productivity drops from 16 sfca/mh to 12 sfca/mh
Assume labor rate equals $30/hr and 5 workers
Damages equal (0.25) ($30) (5 days) (8 hrs/day) (5 workers) = $1,500

FIGURE 9-6 Total Cost Method Example

Actual Project Labor Hours to Place 1,000 units of
    work   =   650 mh

Estimated Project Labor Hours to Place 1,000 units of
    work   =   480 mh

Difference   170 mh

    Times Project Labor Rate $30.00/hr

    Equals Total Claim Damage $5,100.00

The total cost method is the most frequently used method for quantifying lost productivity. This is probably because the method can be used after the fact, even when the project is complete. Given the fact that many firms don't get serious about a problem until late in the project, it follows that the total cost method is frequently utilized.

4. Industrial Engineering Approach

In this approach, industrial engineering models such as time study and work sampling are used to measure productivity impact as it occurs. While this approach represents the most scientific method, it seldom is used. For one, the approach requires the contractor to be knowledgeable about various industrial engineering models. Secondly, the method or approach assumes that the contractor documents the problem as it happens.

5. Earned Value Method

In the Earned Value Method, the calculation of added labor hours is determined by comparing (for select time periods) the hours it took to do a group of activities versus the budgeted hours (or earned hours) for the activities. To illustrate the Earned Value Method, consider the sample project described in Figure 9-7 that represents the planned work durations, planned workdays, planned man-hours relative to the actual durations, and workdays.

FIGURE 9-7 Sample Project Data for Earned Value Method Example

Activity	Planned Duration	Planned Work Days	Planned Man-hours	Planned MH/Day & Crew	Actual Duration	Actual Work Days	Actual Man-hours	Actual MH/ Day & Crew
A	4	1-4	128	32-4	4	10-13	148	37-4.6
B	6	1-6	288	48-6	6	1-6	192	32-4
C	2	1-2	64	32-4	2	5-6	60	30-3.75
D	6	5-10	240	40-5	6	14-16,18-20	290	48.3-6+
E	12	7-18	384	32-4	13	7-19	424	32.6-4+
F	12	3-14	288	24-3	12	7-18	328	27.3-3.4
G	4	19-23	160	40-5	4	20-23	154	38.5-4.8
H	4	23-26	192	48-6	3	24-26	180	60-7.5
I	2	23-24	128	64-8	2	25-26	118	59-7.4
J	8	23-26	256	32-4	7	20-26	280	40-5
Total			2,128				2,174	

Assume the planned schedule per the contractor's submitted "As-planned Schedule" was as follows in Figure 9-8.

Let us further assume that for reasons outside the control and responsibility of the contractor, labor productivity impact occurred during days 11 through 20. Let us further assume that for whatever reason, project activities are delayed and shifted and

FIGURE 9-8 As-planned Schedule

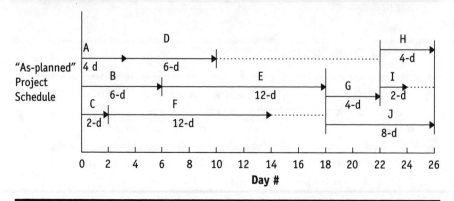

the "As-built" project schedule for the above-illustrated project is as shown in Figure 9-9.

Assuming the contractor has kept track of the actual man-hours expended every day (from the timecards), the lost productivity or man-hours calculated using the Earned Value Method are as shown in Figure 9-10.

The "earned man-hours" for each time period is calculated through a linear interpolation of the time in the impact period. For example, for activity B, the planned or estimated man-hours were 288. The actual duration for activity B was six days. Therefore, each day when B was performed or worked, 48 hours were earned (i.e. 288/6). The "actual man-hours" for each time period would come from the timecards for that time period.

The calculations above for the sample project result in a determination of 175 lost man-hours (productivity) owing to the impact issues. Note that this is higher than the total man-hour overrun of 30 man-hours for the project. The reason is that in time periods outside the "impact period," the contractor actually beats their budget; i.e. had a gain in productivity. As such, the analysis for the sample project shown above indicates that the contractor should be reimbursed for the 175 man-hours (productivity) that he or she lost during the impact period.

FIGURE 9-9 As-built Project Schedule

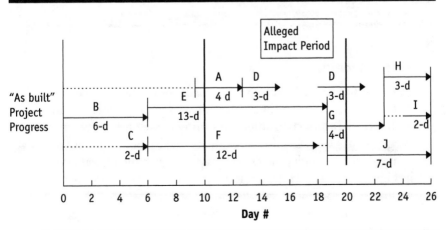

FIGURE 9-10 Earned Value Calculations

Day	Actual Hours	Earned Hours	Lost Hours (Productivity)
1	32	48	(16)
2	32	48	(16)
3	32	48	(16)
4	32	48	(16)
5	62	80	(18)
6	62	80	(18)
7	60	53.5	6.5
8	60	53.5	6.5
9	60	53.5	6.5
10	93	85.5	7.5
11	93	85.5	7.5
12	93	85.5	7.5
13	93	85.5	7.5
14	108.2	93.5	14.7
15	108.2	93.5	14.7
16	108.2	93.5	14.7
17	60	53.5	6.5
18	60	53.5	6.5
19	81	69.5	11.5
20	126.8	116.6	10.2
21	126.8	116.6	10.2
22	78.5	76.6	1.9
23	78.5	76.6	1.9
24	100	100.6	(0.6)
25	159	164.6	(5.6)
26	159	164.6	(5.6)
Total	**2158**	**2128**	

6. Expert Approach

In this approach, a productivity expert reviews the project conditions, project correspondence, and project documentation, and applies industry productivity knowledge and data to the alleged issues to determine a reasonable lost-labor-productivity damage. For example, the expert may reference the information in Figure 9-11 as presenting industry data regarding productivity loss as a function of various impact factors.

Obviously, when using the expert approach, the calculations and the calculated labor cost damages are only as credible

FIGURE 9-11 Example of Expert Analysis of Lost Productivity

Description	Range of impact on productivity per industry publications	Severity on example project	Estimated impact on example project	Onsite labor hours during relevant time frame	Calculation of expected lost labor hours
Weather/ temperature	(10-30%)	small	10%	820	82.0
Inadequate scheduling	(5-15%)	severe	15%	940	141.0
Inadequate supervision	(10-25%)	average	16%	244	39.0
Worker morale	(5-30%)	significant	25%	128	32.0
Interference by other trades	(10-30%)	small	10%	540	54.0
Inadequate skills of workers	(10-30%)	significant	28%	98	27.4

as the individual expert who has reviewed the issues and documents and made the calculations.

In presenting the lost productivity dispute or claim component, it may be advantageous for the supervisor to utilize more than one of the above-described methods for quantifying the lost labor productivity. If two or more methods yield similar results, it may validate the calculations one obtains via the use of a single method.

A Safe Job is a Productive Job

Construction accidents have become so commonplace that they often are taken for granted. Most people view the construction industry as one characterized by dangerous working conditions, accidents, and high costs related to these accidents. The acceptance of these views has reflected negatively on the image of the industry and the willingness of individuals to enter the industry.

Relative to all other industries, the construction industry has the highest incidence rate of accidents:

$$\text{Incidence Rate} = \frac{(\text{Number of injuries} \times 200,000)}{\text{Total worker hours worked in time period}}$$

(Where 200,000 is the base for 100 full time equivalent workers working 40 hours per week, 50 weeks per year.)

Construction accidents often are severe and lead to deaths or disabling injuries. The incidence rate for the construction industry varies from year to year but typically is around 14, as opposed to all other industries' numbers, which are about half of this rate. For an example year, the National Safety Council statistics are as follows:

	Construction	All Industries
Number of workers	5,900,000	116,400,000
(5% of total is construction)		
Deaths	1,800	9,900
(18% of total is construction)		
Disability injuries	180,000	1,700,000
(10.6% of total is construction)		

It should be noted that construction accounted for 1,800 of the total 9,900 work-related deaths in the example (approximately 18 percent). As illustrated above, while the number of deaths is 18 percent of the total, the number of workers in construction accounted for only 5 percent of the total workers in all industries.

While the data shown above are for the entire construction industry, including residential, commercial, and heavy construction, the data are representative of the residential construction industry. Another way to look at the high accident, death, and disabling rates in construction is to view it as a percentage of the work performed.

While construction accidents and deaths have been reduced somewhat over the years, the reductions have been minimal. According to the National Safety Council, the number of deaths and the death rate for the construction industry in 1982 was approximately what it is today.

Cost of Accidents to the Residential Builder

The true cost of accidents leading to death or injury in the construction industry is impossible to measure because one cannot put a price or cost on the victim of a fatality or on his or her loved ones. In addition, when an individual is permanently injured, how can one measure, in money, the individual's loss of mobility or ability to have a normal, unrestricted life? These points aside, the cost of construction accidents include the following:

1. Workers' compensation costs related to insuring against accidents
2. Medical costs

3. Litigation costs for administration and resolution of issues related to the accident
4. Lost worker time
5. Lost labor productivity as workers take added precautions because of the accident
6. Lost labor productivity due to lower worker morale caused by the existence of accidents
7. Direct costs from remedying the worksite after the accident (for example, the need to reconstruct broken scaffolding)

The costs of items E, F, and G are difficult to quantify; however, they do occur. When an accident results in a worker being killed or seriously injured, the accident can have a negative impact on the attitude of fellow workers and supervisors.

While some of the costs related to accidents are difficult to measure, others are not. One of the most obvious costs of accidents relates to the high workers' compensation costs that characterize the construction industry. Workers' compensation costs are a function of the following:

1. Type work. Some construction work is more difficult and subject to a higher risk of accidents.1.
2. Type of labor skill or craft. Some labor crafts do work that is more difficult and subject to a higher risk of accidents.
3. Accident record of the firm.
4. Rates established in various states. Each state has its own workers' compensation laws, and rates vary from state to state.

Owing to the industry's poor safety history, workers' compensation rates for the construction industry average much higher than they are in other industries. These high rates directly affect the residential builders' profit margins.

A Productive Job can be a Safe Job and Vice Versa

More often than not, a productive job can be a safe job. A worker is as likely or more likely to get hurt when he is nonproductive versus when he is performing productive work. A worker in a state of boredom or in a lackadaisical state may find his mind wandering and be careless to the point that he puts himself in an accident-prone situation. An effective safety program that complies with safety regulations and promotes safety to the workers is compatible with the firm's productivity improvement program.

In an attempt to make workers productive, the residential builder should be careful not to overwork or overstress a worker. Each and every worker has the ability to take on a certain amount of work and expend a certain amount of energy in a given time period. If a worker is asked to expend too much energy in a given time period, he or she will become fatigued and is more likely to have an accident. In addition, if the worker is fatigued, he or she also is likely to be less productive.

Workers should be encouraged to lift materials properly, to use equipment when available, and to be cautious that they do not exhaust themselves. A case in point is overtime. There is considerable research available on the impact of extended work hours on the productivity output of a worker. And while less data is available on how overtime affects worker safety, requesting workers to work long hours of overtime clearly enhances the possibility of accidents and safety problems. The point to be stressed is that productivity improvements should not be sought at the expense of safety. Safety and productivity should and can go hand in hand. Working safe is working smart, and working smart is working productively!

Attempts to Reduce Accidents:
The Occupational Safety and Health Administration

The Occupational Safety and Health Administration (OSHA) was created in 1971 in an attempt to stem the tide of an increasing number of accidents in U.S. industries, including the construction industry. OSHA guides attempt to increase safety and reduce accidents via the following:

1. Educating workers on what safety features must be in place to prevent accidents.
2. Accident surveillance and auditing aimed at enforcement of regulations.
3. Penalties and fines related to noncompliance.

4. Research aimed at new technology, tools, and safeguards to be implemented to reduce accidents.

The residential builder is subject to OSHA laws and should take steps to make sure that all employees understand OSHA safety regulations. Knowing what causes accidents and taking measures to avoid them helps reduce safety problems and should be an important component of the residential builders' safety and productivity programs.

Continuous Improvement and Total Quality Management Approach to Construction Safety

There is little doubt that OSHA has had the effect of reducing the number of injuries in the construction industry. However, the accident rate, the number of deaths resulting from the accidents, and the number of disabling accidents remains too high and unacceptable. If the number of accidents, deaths, and disabling accidents are to be reduced significantly, perhaps attention must focus on the behavioral characteristics of the worker that has had an accident. In addition, an approach aimed at studying the cause of the accident may be effective in developing a more aggressive means of analyzing and reducing construction accidents.

In a previous chapter on defect analysis to improve construction productivity emphasis, reference was made to continuous improvement cycle of problem solving with a focus on uncovering the cause of a defect. In a similar approach to accident reduction, when an accident occurs, the residential builder should attempt to gather data regarding the behavioral characteristics of the workers involved in the accident and also the characteristics of the accident. For example, the firm might try to collect data about the following:

1. Age of worker involved in accident
2. Type and amount of prior training the worker has had
3. Marital status of the worker
4. Amount of experience the worker had doing the type of work that was being performed when the accident occurred
5. Type of instructions the worker was given about the work being performed

6. Whether or not the worker was supervised when the accident occurred
7. Whether or not the worker has a prior history of accidents

The concept is fairly simple: by analyzing these and other characteristics of the workers involved in the accident, the residential builder may be able to identify worker characteristics, which "caused" the accident. For example, if the firm finds that many workers are getting involved in an accident after they have been doing repetitive work for a long period of time, the firm could try to rotate the work to avoid this possible cause of accidents. Similarly, if an analysis indicates that workers who have not had training in the last six months are having many accidents, the firm should make an effort to provide them with updated training. The idea is that by removing the cause of the accident, the number of accidents should decrease.

Studying the type of injury as a function of the working conditions may also lead to discovering the cause of the accident. For example, the accident may relate to one of the following issues or causes (listed in order of frequency)

- Falls
- Struck by object *
- Electrical shock
- Caught in/or between
- Explosions/fire
- Cardiovascular/respiratory

By analyzing the frequency of these "causes" of accidents and by combining this analysis with the behavior characteristics of the worker involved, the supervisor should be able to detect the situations or working conditions that led to the accident. By addressing these conditions, the "cause" can be remedied, and the result should be fewer accidents.

There is also a benefit to studying the trends and variations in the number of accidents as a function of time. For example, if the analysis of accident data indicates significant variation from one year to the next in regards to the accidents that were the result of "falls," this variation somewhat infers that if correct actions or precautions are taken, these types of accidents can be reduced or eliminated. On the other hand, a similar analysis might indicate that the number of accidents that were caused by explosion/fires were almost the same each and every year. It may follow that these types of accidents are somewhat inherent to the construction process itself and as such are difficult to reduce or eliminate.

The point is that one cannot be passive in regarding construction accidents. The residential builder should attempt to study the reasons for accidents, not just react to them. By reducing the number and severity of construction accidents, the residential builder will be able to avoid project disruptions, unplanned costs, and negative personnel attitudes that relate to the accidents. A productive job can be attained only if safety is emphasized and achieved. Working smarter, not harder, is compatible with productivity improvements and safety objectives.

Endnotes

1. Maslow, A.H., *A Theory of Human Motivation*, New York, McGraw-Hill, 1969.
2. Herzberg, F., *The Motivation to Work,* New York, Wiley, 1959.
3. Committee on Work in Industry, National Research Council, *Fatigue of Workers: Its Relation to Industrial Production*, New York, Reinhold Publishing Company.